salmonpoetry

Lost Addresses
New & Selected Poems

DIANN BLAKELY

Published in 2017 by
Salmon Poetry
Cliffs of Moher, County Clare, Ireland
Website: www.salmonpoetry.com
Email: info@salmonpoetry.com

ISBN 978-1-910669-56-3

COVER IMAGE: *Tree Woman* – Photo collage by Alexander C. Kafka, incorporating an image in the Commons by Karl Struss.

COVER DESIGN & BOOK TYPESETTING: *Siobhán Hutson*

Printed in Ireland by Sprint Print

Acknowledgments

for *Fragments of a Requiem: New Poems:*

Avatar Review, "Fragments of a Requiem, No. 13" (2013); *Cimarron Review*, "Invitation" (forthcoming); *Malpais Review*, "Cottonwoods, San Antonio" (forthcoming); *Mezzo Cammin*, "Another Art," "Charlotte Brontë's Gloves," and "Santa Ana" (Winter 2012-2013); *New South*, "Jailbird" and "The Window Seat" (Vol. 3, No. 2, Summer 2010); *New World Writing*, "The Story of Their Lives" and "Two Collects" (Summers 2012-2013); *Oxford American*, "Vesper Sparrow" (Summer 2010); *Shenandoah*, "Elegiac Fragments: A Quartet" (Spring 2014).

Aside from those named directly in its pages, this book is dedicated with humility and gratitude to those guides—Nin Andrews, Frederick Barthelme, Kim Bridgford, Alfred Corn, Steve Harris, Quincy R. Lehr, Suzanne Lummis, Bruce Smith, R.T. Smith, Richard Tillinghast, and Baron Wormser—who believed in new directions before I even glimpsed them; and to my teachers—including the late Donald Davie, Donald Justice, and William Matthews; also Vereen Bell, Susan Mitchell, and Ellen Bryant Voigt—who positioned me when I was still more than half-blind and stumbling. "The Window Seat" remains reserved for Stanley Booth. And, with more than appreciation always, to Anne Delana Reeves and AWW.

for *Selected Poems*:

These poems originally appeared in my first three books: *Hurricane Walk* (BOA Editions, Ltd., 1992), *Farewell, My Lovelies* (Story Line, 2000), and *Cities of Flesh and the Dead* (Elixir Press, 2008). I offer my appreciative thanks to the publications in which these poems originally appeared, sometimes in earlier versions. Several have been selected for reprint: "Antonioni's *Blow-Up*," *Dublin Poetry Review*, ed. Hélène Cardona; "Magi" and "Georgia Pilgrimage," *The Enchanting Verses Literary Review*, guest ed. Hélène Cardona; "History," *Irresistible Sonnets and The Southern Poetry Anthology*, Vol. VI, Tennessee, ed. Mary Meriam and eds. William Wright, Jesse Graves, and Paul Ruffin (Texas Review Press, 2013); "Memphis Blues," *Lost in the Forest* (http://rosekelleher.wordpress.com/2013/07/23/memphis-blues-by-diann-blakely); "Chorale," "Reunion Banquet, Class of '79," and "The Storm," *Levure Litteraire*, guest ed. Hélène Cardona; "Duplex Noir," *The Malpais Review*; "Reunion Banquet, Class of '79," *The Movies: Texts, Receptions, Exposures*, eds. Laurence Goldstein and Ira Konigsberg (University of Michigan Press, 1996) as well as *Lights, Camera, Poetry!*, ed. Jason Shinder (Harcourt Brace, 1998); "Before the Flood: A Solo From New Orleans," *Pushcart Prize Anthology XX*, ed. Carol Muske-Dukes.

Deep gratitude to Diann Blakely's estate, Hillary Stringfellow, Rodney Jones, Blas Falconer, Julie Kane, Denise Duhamel, Hélène Cardona, Kendra Hamilton, Ben Downing, Anne Delana Reeves, and Arthur Wadsworth.

Contents

Preface

Taking notes as if the world might disappear
—Diann Blakely

What is it about being white and southern that dooms and exalts, that confabulates narrative and song, and prefers a present always nested inconveniently in a history that is invariably class-bound, masculine, and befogged by the twin monstrosities of religious narrowness and xenophobic bigotry? For Diann Blakely, as for Eleanor Ross-Taylor, Betty Adcock, Ellen Bryant Voigt, and C.D. Wright, these burrs proved less impediments than a mandate for loyal opposition. Her three award-winning books, *Hurricane Walk*; *Farewell, My Lovelies*; and *Cities of the Flesh and the Dead*, spaced eight years apart, should be seen as stations of a complex, aesthetic, political, and religious pilgrimage. *Lost Addresses: New and Selected Poems*, which she was still working on when she died, is her chosen focus, the crystal through which she would be read.

She grew up in Mountain Brook, a wealthy suburb of Birmingham, Alabama in the civil rights era. The images of racial violence on television and the status of the maids in her own household struck a dissonant chord, and, as she matured and traveled, she never got over or denied the unfairness of her genteel privilege. Immodestly Anglican, macaronian in her tastes, unapologetically urbane, a lover of great movies and paintings, of high modernism, of rock'n roll and the dirty, lowdown blues, educated at Sewanee and Vanderbilt, and in classes with Seamus Heaney and Derek Walcott, she was every inch a sophisticated woman of her time. She did not write regional eclogues or idylls, but a poetry of diverse, intellectual reference, and if the casually beheld facts of her biography might tempt some to define her as "the last of the fugitive poets," that suspicion should be allayed by a cultural inclusiveness that does not omit Sid Vicious and Johnny Rotten.

Her vision is complicated, as persons in transit like to say. Helen Keller sits in Mark Twain's lap. Rock stars and poets triage identities. Anna Akhmatova, Flannery O'Connor, El Greco, and Princess Di collide with Jack the Ripper, John Travolta, and Leni Riefenstahl. She embodied in her manner the gentility that she opposed, and the rage that fuels the last lines of "Foucault in Vermont" descends from Birmingham as much as from Simone de Beauvoir and Robert Lowell:

> the greatest pain
> And pleasure are melted into one. De Sade
> And de Chardin. The virus swarms your brain...
> But now this woolen hat. No melting here,
> A state fist-fucked by winter every year.

Through all of *Lost Addresses*, her immediate gift and penchant mark a harmony of lyrical ear and narrative mind in the precise intonation that became her signature. She was underrated in both her ambition and accomplishment. She wrote more effectively in the high register than any southern poet of her generation.

I knew her best in telephone conversations when she lived in the relentless pain of the hereditary lung disease known as Alpha 1 that would bring on her premature end. To speak with her in 2012 and 2013 was mostly to listen to a fine mind striated and muscled by steroids. In the confinement of the house in Brunswick, Georgia, where she lived with her celebrated music writer husband, Stanly Booth, she had started a Facebook Forum, *Notes on the State of Southern Poetry*, in which she sought to engage fellow literary isolates in a supportive literary community. Her description of the group's mission might well describe her own objective: "We seek to explore the cultural multiplicity of places traditionally associated with the American South and the various forms of art created therein; but we wish always to stress national and global connections. All are welcome to join. No exclusivity permitted."

She was not herself in these days, friends said, yet she was, too: quick, nervous, birdlike and brilliant, even when she would not be convinced that my friend Allison Joseph, born in London of Afro-Caribbean parents and reared in the Bronx, was not, in fact, a Southern poet.

No one loved poetry more or was more intolerant of pretension, yet she was shy about claiming her own place. She characterized herself as a semi-formalist, but her aesthetic was eclectic, bold, and far-ranging. She believed in *le mot juste*, in measure and music, was a master of the sonnet and villanelle, but also experimented with a longer, wilder line and worked for many years on a still unpublished book, *Rain in Our Door: Duets with Robert Johnson*, which may well prove the ultimate white southerner's poem that attempts to cross the great racial divide, join the chamber band to the blues ensemble, and, in a direct political sense, enact an aesthetic and cultural unity.

My fear is the common one, that her poetry should be lost. There are ample reasons for a poet to be neglected, temporarily submerged in a trend, or permanently effaced, for poetry is a cold media and the music that the claim of poetry rests on may not always be acknowledged. Still Diann Blakely's poetry depends less on what she says—though she says plenty—than the music implicit in the perfect opening sentence of "Opening Credits:" "The six-foot maître d' at Bar Marmont/ Wears a kimono to die for" or the line at the middle of her splendid villanelle, "Another Art:" "The walls warm themselves like dangerous animals." Throughout *Lost Addresses*, such lines stand alone, fierce and joyful, and the reader who listens into her textures will hear the abundant felicity of her singular art. This book is proof against forgetting.

—RODNEY JONES

Fragments of a Requiem:
New Poems

The Story of Their Lives

1. *Tuscumbia, Alabama*

Dense-clustered ivy climbs outside a window
Open as Helen's mouth: she snatches bread
From Mother's plate; her dirty fingers spread
The air, demanding butter. She can't notice

The stars outside, soft and almost fragrant
With Alabama spring, or hear the wind
That lifts the rambling, leafy vine for which
This house is named. Silent, an aproned servant

Brings the stranger into the dining room.
Captain and Mrs. Keller exchange looks
When Boston-Irish Annie starts to speak,
Her accent odd: the garish vowels boom;

Her thick-lensed gaze never leaves their daughter.
Helen, too, knows an alien is present
And revolts: her greased fists strike the parent
Who dotes on "this wild, uncouth little creature"

And plates crash on the mirrory waxed floor.
A lullaby will calm them both to sleep,
The mother thinks. *How sweetly angels weep.*
The captain, who survived the Civil War

And still wears shiny buttons stamped "CSA,"
Removes his butter-smeared reading glasses
And cleans them with a napkin. Disliking chaos,
He starts toward his study, hung with sabers

And a Rebel flag. But Helen charges Annie,
Who spent childhood with whores and pregnant girls
In Tewksbury Almshouse, who dined on gruel
And crusts for years. Who doesn't know this story

Of ill fates mastered, of love and miracles,
Although in future tense? Now Annie slaps
Her shocked new pupil back. "The greatest step
Will be taken when, the Kellers schooled

From all such interference, the little savage
Learns her first lessons in obedience"—
With daily bribes of buttered bread and silk ribbons—
"And finds the yoke easy." But tonight's passage

Is slow as ivy's climb along a trellis
Or the patient, white wing-beats of those angels
Who hover among stars. The child sniffles
Through matted coils of hair, then smashes

Both hands against another window, closed.
(Dear Reader, ivy is no gentle plant
But pulls apart the sturdy granite slabs
Of houses; and once I saw, my own mouth open,

A copperhead, its dull head stuck between
Dry stringy fronds: it struck against a window-
Screen behind which a toddler dozed,
Hot fangs caught in the standard-issue twine.)

Now Father, Mother, dim-sighted Annie stare
At their own wounded shadows, cracked and shattered,
As broken glass drops to the floors, and clatters,
Blood-stained. None dare to look away. None dare.

2. *St. Louis Cathedral, New Orleans*

The brick abrades her fingers. What is that smell?
Now she touches a wrought-iron balcony,
Wipes her hand across her mouth. July is hell

In New Orleans: heat and a death-knell
For twins, coffined and dressed identically.
The brick abrades her fingers. What is that smell,

As heavy with rot as the old well
Where boys at home drown litters of puppies,
Wipe their hands across their mouths? July is hell

When strange perfume and faithless love-sweat spill
Across a thousand sheets—o profane city
Whose brick abrades Helen's fingers. Those smells

Of mud and beer, chicory, the dew on petals
That droop toward the twins' pale cheeks. Too blurry
To understand, the words that Annie spells

Into Helen's hand. Again the death-knell,
And Pupil clutches Teacher, panicky
At the air's strange pulse, but Annie won't tell

What its vibrations mean. Their white skirts tail,
Hems mingled on the sidewalk. *Talk to me.*
Brick abrades Helen's fingers. What is that smell?
She wipes her hand across her mouth. July is hell.

3. Angelfish

"Blindness is an exciting business," says Mr. Twain,
Helen on his lap. But what's more sweetly flagrant
Than hot-breathed courtship from a man so near one's age?
John Macy knocks over the decanted sherry
To kiss Annie's moistening hand. Helen flurries
At Twain's lips, read the words there, now profane—
"Dear one, I must curse." Continuing with talk
His newest pet describes as tobacco-fragrant,

He ignores Annie's moist and much-kissed hand. "Sixteen
Is the dearest and sweetest of all ages." White thatch
Of hair. White-moustached mouth continuing with talk
Of love—"tears and flapdoodle"—as more decantered sherry
Is fetched and served; John quaffs a glass and, slurring
Words, he asks for Annie's hand. But choose between
A man and Helen? She cuts another hunk of cake.
Her pupil's laughter jars. Happy girls, booms Twain,

Will forgo hot-breathed courtship with men their own age.
"Dear one, I must curse." Continuing with talk
Of girls who sweeten his old age, Twain's white thatch tickles
Helen, still on his lap. But what's more sweetly flagrant
Than kisses on one's virgin hand? Sherry-fragrance
Wafts between Annie and John. More chocolate cake.
"To make a perfect and completed whole, it takes
The two of you. Exciting business," says Mr. Twain.

4. Winter Garden Theatre

So eagerly she parts her lips
    Then turns both cheeks for rouging
While this new friend—*Folks, got your tickets?*—
    Advises, for the chilly wings,

A warmer shawl. With greasepaint—
    Come hear Miss Helen Keller speak!—
She'll make the odd-voiced, angel-faced
    (*O where is, where is Peter?*),

And still broken-hearted Helen
    More ethereally gorgeous
At forty than at sweet sixteen.
    Annie's lungs, ravaged

By the TB that's nested there
    Since Tewksbury Almshouse—
And tonight starring Sophie Tucker!—
    Have forced her home to rest

And brood on loss: Johnny's gone.
    At Captain Keller's death,
His widow shipped eight trunks to Wrentham—
    Who'll sing your requests—

And, piece by piece from her garden
    To train New England ivy,
The trellis (*"Where is my true love gone?"*)
    To join her voice with Annie's:

Their Helen mustn't marry. But Sophie—
    The Last of the Hot Mamas!
Cries "Balderdash," her kimono
    Embroidered with feathers

Like the green and blue ones in her hair,
    Untied and flapping, as heat
Begins to clank the radiators.
    "'Tain't vanity to want

The love of a good man, no matter
    What old hens cluck." Their shriek:
"Have you been kissing that creature?"
    (*"O when will he come back?"*)
"His name is Peter, and I love him,"
    Signed Helen, then began
To pack her trunk for the elopement.
    Don't leave—She sat till dawn,

Her fingers on her lips as now
    They rest on Sophie's. Rehearsed
"I love you"s, otherworldly vowels.
    Two acrobats, finished

Performing for the night, announce,
    Sweat sheening their red tights,
The dog act's next: Les Princesses
    From Par-ee! Don't leave your seats!

Sophie checks both their faces
    In the bulb-starry mirror,
Adds more rouge, which drifts to fleck the lace
    Beneath pale Helen's ears,

Fleck the lace like tiny spots
    Of blood. She'd sat till dawn,
Breathed early and unwelcome heat—
    And now, the deaf and blind—

On her face, the stars devoured;
    The first birds beat their feathers
Against sprouting trellis bars—
    Will speak! Where was he, O Reader?

22

5. Westport

But Helen's dreaming of Los Angeles,
The salt winds drift off the still-chilly Sound,
Recalling scents from—the thirties, forties,

Pacific breeze and—which hotel's greens?
Her hands stroked flowers there as Teacher spelled

A trembling skein of consonants and vowels:
"Wisteria." "White jasmine." That nicked stone angel,
Its stare a lidless blank, looked past dropped towels

And trysts then too, as the near-sixty Pupil

Looked past her ailing Teacher's cheek: ivy,
Not jasmine. The thrice-moved, green-choked trellis . . .
Now half-awake, Helen strokes pale signs

On the salt-heavy air. Who can resist
Inscribing on the present (O, Dear Reader,

Read closer, closer!) lines from the past?
And how decades, and their trips, blur:
In which did Chaplin plan that film—the twenties?—

With Helen called Deliverance? The star

Would play a disguised prince; his sleeping beauty,
Whose stepmother, still watchful, had read the script—
"A fairy tale revised!"—and, confusedly,

Felt his kiss steered to her cheek, not lips.
Her hand now strikes gray braids that coil along

Her white nightgown's lace collar. Two sherries sipped
At a much-storied club made Helen long
To dance, till Chaplin asked the band for jazz,

When she clutched Annie: the shadowed pulse of jungles,

Vine-snaked, where she'd been lost. (Ex-savages,
Dear Reader, fear the hot nostalgic lure
Of clenched and blood-stained fists, of rapine

We call desire, its fanged teeth always bared
For alien flesh, mouths wide.) Miss Sullivan

Seemed rattled too: jazz moaned like Tewksbury,
Its wild and daylong chorus of the mad,
The pregnant girls who wept in tangled hair

For lives erased by love. Pale Helen's hand

Clutched Teacher's in smoke-murky air. In air
Now present tense and salty, again her hand
Moves to her lips and remembers W-A-T-E-R,

The rocking chair, a cake. . . . Dear Reader, spellbound
Or bored with cryptic addresses, bored

With other lives and voices, it's time to loose
This story, to let Helen float away
From Westport, childhood, Los Angeles: you choose

Her resting place. A white headstone, engraved

With letters etched more deeply than her face,
Almost unlined, except for nail-made welts—
The little savage's herself. And less

Of her each year. O Reader, what's the self?
"For me to marry," Helen wrote, "would doom

A man to marrying a statue, as heaven
Has not equipped me equally." She smoothes
The rumpled sheets, knowing love's bargain;

And angels, seeing her white gown, and, too,

Those blankly staring eyes, are sure all things
Belong to them, as crowds and her loved two?—
Or three? Or four?—were sure. A cherub sings.

to Lisa Russ Spaar and Jeanie Thompson

Invitation

O come be hot elsewhere than New York:
Your cratered, sun-jackhammered sidewalk
Won't forbid more ravage, cab-exhaust,
The dull cursed drops from each brow and armpit
Or furnace blasts from burning subway vents
That melt plastic sandals off feet in seconds.
Come visit soon. I'll pretend the AC's
On the blink, the merest window-breeze
Should make you lust for exile: dear, how long
Since you've grown breathless just by raising
An iced tea glass, or watched mold lush and ooze
Like the backyard's hysteria of kudzu,
Its silent growth in hours from feet to lips?
Our hands will travel like apocalypse.

Santa Ana

The scrub pines burn like matchsticks, the houses tinder
When fall's dry winds howl through the desert
And pound on redwood doors. Fixing dinner,

Meek wives take carving knives from kitchen drawers
And eye their husbands' necks. What's for dessert
When scrub pines burn like matchsticks, the houses tinder?

Your husband's nightly beers and Raymond Chandler,
Who wrote of knives and the flesh they hurt,
Rage pounding at redwood doors. Fixing dinner,

You phone a friend in Long Beach: her breasts are sore
But larger. Today she bought some new tight white shirts
Though scrub pines burned like matchsticks, the houses tinder

On her drive to Rodeo. When husbands wander
As if blown by hot gales, some wives, still sutured,
Pound at redwood doors. Or fix dinner,

Pretend nothing's wrong, and grow thinner.
"Get pregnant," your friend says. "Buy a new hat."
The scrub pines burn like matchsticks, the houses tinder.
She pounds at redwood doors. You fix dinner.

Opening Credits

The six-foot maître d' at Bar Marmont
Wears a kimono to die for—jade green
Embroidered with red and black dragons
Whose lifted tails repeat the well-plucked sheen

    Of his eyebrows. Repeat the curving waves
    Slammed lavishly against the gull-pocked jetties;
    Also tiny waves sloshed from glass to table.
    Campari, ice cubes, foam. Whose face is pretty

When pocked and sloshed with tears? Here's your compact.
Here's your comb. Small marvels: a clean tissue
And favorite lipstick. Should you have nipped and tucked?
Love's death is no one's fault, but like fissures

    Left by earthquakes, like the walls of houses
    Slashed from canyons by mud, needs a scapegoat.
    You need another drink. Your weekend's hosts,
    Both native-born, are late. Applaud the drag act

Of the maître d' with a large tip.
His maquillage's to die for too, but where's
The wig and fake cleavage? The padded hips?
How often you've applauded late-show stars

    Who fake death to escape it: one open eye,
    Or black-lashed flutter on a pancaked cheek,
    Tells you that the plucky star's alive
    Though mud-pocked and bleeding at a man's feet,

Embroidering his shoes; curved breasts peek through
The slashed kimono. Fake husbands can't survive
Without wives' dividends, without their new,
Much younger loves. You've repeated their lines

In favorite nightmares, also to your friends:
Both lifted their eyebrows. *Why not move here?*
Too thin, too pale? Land of eternal tans:
Love ends with tears; death, a drag, lingers.

to Molly Bendall

Another Art

Voicelessness. The snow has no voice.
The walls, also, seem to be warming themselves,
My heart opens and closes: awareness,

Or protection, month after month, to no purpose?
In Munich, morgue between Rome and Paris,
Voicelessness reigns. The snow has no voice,

And I have wanted to efface myself. Tulips
Forced open in the domesticity of windows!
The walls warm themselves like dangerous animals,

But mannequins lean in their furs, orange lollies
Where light slowly widens and slowly thins.
The walls, also, seem to be warming themselves

Where the yew trees blow like sulfur hydras
Or the fanged mouths of great African cats,
If not where snow drops its pieces of darkness.

Why bother to keep the bureaus and tea sets,
Or months, tamped shoes, Stolzes, orange lollies—
All voiceless! The snow has no voice,
But my heart opens: why close awareness?

Advent: A Collect

Break-in and battery two weeks before the season's grand hallelujah: broken glass from a shat-tered window wreathed her body, found below in the tub. Did the pills let her creep there, as if searching for a manger, a word ringing with "safety"? Usually afraid—a grandfather's multiple rapes—to shower or bathe alone, what else could have eased this blood-stained pilgrimage, ropes trailing around her wrists and ankles as though she were a half-opened gift? Lord, let me pluck a sole skein-like straw of understanding. Let the drugs that thrummed in her system have black-ened the room and all sense so that she felt nothing in those pre-dawn Christmas hours. Saw no rising Eastern star through the jagged window pane or suffered Thy cold breath on her frosted, bluing skin. *Amen.*

Charlotte Brontë's Gloves

Hands lower to touch that wedding dress
And silk-draped hat on Jane Eyre's bed.
Beyond windows, what should be the dead
Of winter comforts us with moony pollens,
A few blossoms on mostly still-bare limbs.
Last week's snow melts. "Reader, I married him."

Also last week, a stunt pilot's fiery crash
Consumed five houses only blocks from here.
Black jacket, silk gloves. Did he know *Jane Eyre*?
You want me to stop reading, get undressed,
Four hundred pages and just one real joke:
I flip back to the house where Brock-

lehurst—a cruel, vicious minister—quizzes
The orphaned Jane on hell. What must she do
To avoid the demon-heated stew
Of fumes and ash? Forswear the body's lusts?
"I must keep in good health, sir, and not die."
Silk sheets, your winter-leathered hands on mine:

To rebuild one house? Her gloves on show.
The pilot looped and swirled to spell out
A message. "Jane loves Eddie," he wrote
In letters pale as those blossoms the moon shadows,
As my own hands, reclutching this book.
And what of poor Bertha, escaped from the attic?

She'd grown too mad to inscribe her portraits
On virginal white paper. And with words.
In just a few hours, befuddled birds
Flown back too soon from Florida marshes,
Will sing back-up for the dawn, its red flames
Burning the sky. Should I have changed my name

When we married, long ago? (To digress
Is human, to forgive, divine.) How long
Till you'll be blind with sleep, bent arm tingling
With the blood pooled and vein-congested?
A girl from the tropics, I miss the sun
But love, like Charlotte Brontë, to read till dawn;

And once I loved to touch you, my hands gloveless
And burning with cold. O remember how
We traipsed across the moors, and kissed? And now
I want to rebuild this winter-battered house:
An attic bedroom, warmed by a fireplace,
New bookshelves, where mirrors hold both faces.

An Aviary

What is most underrated about the South? The regionally, if often unconsciously, shared belief in original sin. Responsible for hellfire-and-damnation sermons, bigotry, intolerance, and xenophobia, this traditional Christian doctrine nonetheless allows even professed atheists to agree that being human equals being fundamentally flawed and thus being capable of inexplicable, even horrific, actions; that all souls have their strong points and their weak ones; and that most of us are doing the best we can. On the other hand (e.g., the Misfit and Popeye), we know that genu-ine evil exists. Or, as Baudelaire and the Louvin Brothers put the matter, "Satan is real."

Vesper Sparrow

Of course you went to the stadium's highest tiers.
Of course you heard the dark and trilling rhyme—
Tears—as flesh began unfeathering from
What you called "your big Dutch bones." Good Friday.
But birds know nothing of Baptist calendars,
Twittering, circling, rising, falling, spiralling
In what, to them, is merely spring, green-edged
In central Massachusetts where Emily,
Fleet and avian—"my eyes are like the wren's"—
Lived, where her poems first outlived her. A flock!
A covey! A murmuration cushioning your
Last descent to earth, where, when last
We talked, you ground a cigarette beneath
Your heel and said, "Let's get this over with."
You meant a reading of your poems. O "Rock,
Scissors, Paper," its swirling congeries
Of Darwin, Freud, and Marx. Good luck to you,
Sweet vesper sparrow! "Good-luck, good-luck, good-luck."
Know that the birds you loved now soften their nests
With smashed—but surely—fresh-brushed hair. Your own.

i.m. Deborah Digges

The Window Seat

Here's country, perhaps, for aging men
And their sick wives. Your spine broken
To shards, and I with my bad lungs
Watch coastal suns, mist–blurred, carve rungs
In Georgia sky, already hot
In May, at least by noon. And not
Just suns but birds. How late we've come
To dawn's bright side, to bites of rum
In our *cafés au lait*, to love
And birds themselves. And so we'll rove
With rock stars and with poets who
Triage identities—they do—
No more but stay well stocked with seeds
For finches, painted buntings, red-
Winged blackbirds. Squirrels we bang away
To keep their needled teeth at bay.

Jailbird

Where to migrate, after the South of France,
With so many outstanding U.S. warrants
On your head that you'd be manacled
As soon as you stepped off the plane. O exile.
O vodka, Oxycontin, Ambien
And benzos too. I knew they'd cage you in.
How idiotic I was to think writing
Would set you free. But so did you, trifling
With the language, with your talent for words
That often overwhelmed their subjects' chords.
Let's go back to New York City—or no,
New Orleans, brass-knuckled jazz and zydeco.
Nothing like this dirge-filled silence. July.
My friend, I hope your soul, unfettered, flies.

i.m. Bernard Patrick

Cottonwoods, San Antonio

Dusk-chilled October wind rustles through silver leaves
    By this downtown *paseo*, and my friend tells me
That trees here thrive on little rain, that it's not safe

To stay past dark. We fill in gaps left by letters
    Since she came west to take that job: scattershot talk,
No mention of the child she lost years back. Below,

On the river, sombreroed guides steer red barges
    And point out landmarks, lilt their stories amid swirls
Of glittering leaves, but this town has other stories,

Ones my friend tells me, of barrio midnights cracked
    By gunfire, of sidewalks sprayed with knife-pierced crosses
Or skulls wreathed with roses. *Paseo de Rio*,

Where cottonwoods border the brick walk's edge, their trunks
    Protected by wire. *Alamo*—the Spanish word
For this poplar whose branches, in spring, sprout pale tufts.

And I'm surprised to find the famous mission small,
    Its façade crumbled; inside, a glass case displays
Colonel Travis's letter, its flourished postscript

The Lord is on our side. Alamo—"cottonwood,"
    Abundant in the state whose name comes from tejas,
"Friend," and mine's left her job in the neighborhood school,

Burned out after a mission she hoped would redeem
    Those crippled by bullets, the pregnant twelve-year-olds
Who find their front doors bolted, that crack-manic scream

With a flicked-open switchblade during a lesson
    On the state's most notorious battle, warning
Anglo bitch. What can I say, here for a weekend,

Recalling my cheery letters—*She'd turn seven*
  This year, she says—as arrogant with platitudes
As Travis's, enshrined in glass while night slams down

On the façade? That history, hope too, are suffered
  With fewer resources than the bare cottonwoods,
Roots spiking dust beneath wind-keening, ashen leaves?

Divorce: A Collect

Lord, he called me a snake and our marriage invalid because performed by a bear and a sexually predatory priest. Let me interrupt my prayer unto Thee: it wasn't a bear, but a judge who loved safaris and filled his chambers with taxidermied trophies, one ursine. As for snakes, yes, I wear a dia-mond cloak and admire my own litheness of spine, coil and recoil through this world on my bel-ly, feeling vibrations—like coming footsteps—and I rise to bite the heels which would tread on me. Why are the fangs that fill and glisten then pop, sharpened, through my mouth's pink roof always ascribed to a male version of me? I may not be the apple of anyone's eye—except Eve's, hungry for girl-talk—but pumped venom should be prized if it brings souls closer to Thee. Or say the Word only, and I shall protect us from any further thudding of bodies and purge the world with Our venomous song. *Amen.*

to Holle Weiss-Friedman

Fragments of a Requiem, No. 13

1. Prelude: A Memorial Service, 1997

Grief turns mascara to black ink,
　　Turns girlhood friends to furies
Whose rose-lipped mouths open to sing
The Kaddish.　My heart translates *o murder*;

Translates *O Lord our God of Israel,*
　　Smite all false-hearted men
Who dream of divorce, or their wives killed;
Let lightning torch their flesh, their hands

Melt to black blood.　Grief turns their faces
　　To their children's, unsmudged
After washcloths and soap.　Translate,
Scarred heart, *o law*, translate *o Judge*

While the police search joggers' trails,
　　The ice-etched, tree-walled ponds
In parks.　And drag the river's roil
The way these mothers dragged wet combs

Through tangles in their children's hair,
　　Most darker than my own.
The keening turns; and now I hear
O weep for how we never left home

But packed the generations with towels
　　And sheets, the broken glass
Saved with our wedding veils.　For exile
To faces growing lined and slack,

To knowledge torn from a friend's slaughter.
　　Should outsiders turn where—
O Lost One, artist, wife, and mother—
The men's heads bow to offer prayers

That they weren't born to be romanced
    By late shows, or to bleed.
O weep that lives we once imagined
Have disappeared like her dead body—

No one knows how. Just miles away,
    The police search, once more,
Woods near the missing's house for graves.
Why have I come here? Where's the door?

2. *"Yellow Taxi": Post-Mortem, 2000*

Above her signature, the huge cab bulks
In front of shop windows rose-gray with dusk
And emptied of their mannequins. A lake,

Or pond, spreads humid wind among the horns
Blown by stalled tourists, the pre-showtime diners
And downtown bosses en route to happy hours . . .

Where's the cab driver? Where's the painting?—hung
In this swank bar. "The guilty husband hangs,"
Predicts one guy, who knew Janet when young

And winning preschool stars for what she drew.
"I like artistic types," he winks. "Like you."
I sip vodka, teeth rattled by the ice cubes,

And then reject his proffered coat to shiver,
Though it's now June. The painting—where's the driver?—
Exudes a sweaty glow; my next rejoinder

Sounds both vaguely flirtatious and unkind.
No metaphoric stab will close my wounds.
Too long alone, I dream nightly of bones

Or read, past midnight, Akhmatova's great lines
For women bowed, death-still as mannequins,
At windows where they asked if beloved sons . . .

"Buy you a drink?" This chance encounter wants
Two boys some day. And me? Two blaring sirens.
A cab, but steered by my two ringless hands.

3. *Epithalamion, 2011*

It's thirteen years since my divorce; thirteen
Times three beloveds gone, and six proved keen
To join them: in my new household, we maintain

A running body count and dye our jeans

And shirts in mourning. Now, post-Easter dawn,
What occasion fits, to speak in puns,
Better to rewind a tape in crumbs

Of obsequies before a royal union,

The shots crosshatched? So to speak, again:
Poor Akhmatova, whose only son
Disliked her once she set him free, thus and

Asunder? O how we hate—and love—imprison-

Ers, and those who loose their very hands
From our pale fragile throats? Again, again:
What is life if not repetition,

And sentences, or lines, for those sullen

With crafts and arts? So let me stop,
Reject all rhyme, near, perfect, slant,
And tell the worn-out truth: this, as pops,

On our TV, a fuzzed recording, and:

4. *Love Lies Bleeding, 1997 and 2011*

Wrought iron and gold, the palace gates swing wide
As the cortège begins its procession
Through sun-hushed London streets, a hush broken
Too quickly by a woman's high-pitched cry,

A single lung-torn note repeated till
It translates as mine. Black horse-hooves clop.
TV reporters, for a moment, drop
Their glossy anecdotes about the ball

Or photo-op where the Princess spoke
To them, alone. A moment when the soul
Weeps for all lost addresses. Like the cul-
De-sac where Buckingham bulks gray; or like

The lane where Janet's dream house, a stone dacha,
Stood empty when the detectives and lawyers
Removed her paintings, though not the porch's flowers
Once left in tribute; or Akhmatova's

St. Petersburg apartment where she wrote
To translate her keening into a nation's.
"Di read cheap romances, a real bird brain,"
My ex-belovèd offered on the phone;

"The two of you had nothing more in common
Than a nickname," which failed to stop my tears.
I'd made him late, and for the same firm dinner
Where we'd once sat by Janet—"spoiled past rotten,"

My unkind verdict—and his colleague, wedged
Between, "a jerk." Now jailed. Free to weep for
Something beyond my heart's four puny chambers,
I lipstick words on my own mirror's edge

And glimpse no lasting scars. I'm free to sing,
To mourn and yet take joy, to bow in church
And ask that words, transformed by prayer, can stanch
A child's tears, or a people's. To bleed and sing,

For we're all silent at that last address,
The grave's temple, though some are offered tributes
Of farewell notes and bouquets. Offered pop tunes:
"Goodbye English Rose." Goodbye to Janets, Annas,

To all the banished princesses of lives
Reprised like Heaven's favorite song. Lives spent
Between the castle and the prison gate,
God's terrified exiles. Or law's. Or love's.

i.m. Eleanor Ross Taylor

Translations: A Memory Play

QUINCE
Bless thee, Bottom, bless thee. Thou art translated.
A Midsummer Night's Dream

Just past midsummer's eve, that wild night
Inhabited by fairies, by lovers who blink
And find themselves drawn to another's kiss,
That wild night inspiring tulled embraces,
Those en pointe arabesques and fish-tailed plunges
Dizzying as brews the druids boiled in vats,
Fermenting mixtures of berries and leaves
That probably smelled like heat-waved Broadway

At the post-matinée hour. Lovelier, Balanchine's
Pink world of elves and sprites, lovers who blink
And switch tracks faster than New York's subways,
Their riders who avoid each other's glances
In stifling cars sparking at speeds
Dizzying as brews the druids brewed in vats
As thick as that district's once-famed baths
Where naked men caressed each other

In fluid anonymity. O waters of longings—
Switching currents faster than New York's subways—
Wet and salt as tears. The parade's hilarity
Seethes down Christopher, and you emerge,
Headed home, deeply vertiginous still
As if you'd been in that district's once-famed baths
Instead of watching Titania's *fouettés*,
Her tiaraed head snapping back with each kick

To find its focal point. And now you blink—
Sweat, not tears—at the parade's hilarity
And are scrutinized by a tutued man
Fluttering a pink-sequinned fan and singing
With the loudspeakers: *could this be the magic?*

Instead of watching Titania's *fouettés*,
You watch floats pass like giant confections
And crowds hanging from fire escapes to cheer,

Tiaras slip from wigs on bright shaved heads;
And you're scrutinized by that tutued man,
Pink satin bodice rolled beneath his ribs.
Remember walking home from ballet class,
The playground's boys whooping at your pink tights?
You watch floats pass like giant confections
But also see those boys slam one to concrete,
Hear their circling taunts. *Girl. Pussy.*

Get your mama to buy you a dress.
Pink satin bodice rolled beneath his ribs,
The man lifts his arms—bone-thin, lesioned—
To catch the beads thrown by the next float's riders.
New York's not often home, and you push
To join two boys standing on raised concrete
For a better view. You're all on tiptoe.
Here men call each other *girl* with irony

And love. *Could this be the magic at last?*
The man lifts his pink-lesioned arms
In this habitation of *fairies*, of lovers who blink
And hope they'll be alive when their eyes open.
A blonde queen's stopped to strut her stuff,
And for better views, you're all on tiptoe
In air dizzying as brews the druids boiled in vats:
Someone calls out *girl* and you're twelve again,

And happy. O wild nights of someone else.
Get your mama to buy you a dress.
I did, and solo plane and ballet tickets too—
Could this be the magic at last? I've known long
And miss wild nights of someone else,
That pink slip dress I once wore on the street,
Expelled post-love, then that matinée.
Girl. Pussy. Fag. Fairy. Welcome nowhere, I'm home.

                    to Erica Dawson

Elegiac Fragments: A Quartet

Did you like slasher flicks, their doomed coeds
In eighties leg-warmers, six-packed dates
Loaded for a weekend's fun with sex and sleds

And skis? But not in the Magnolia State,
Where rows runnel the delta's silt, not snow,
Seeds scattered like mascara-flecks on Kate,

Kimmie, eyes taking on a raccoon's glow,
Or madmen's, who pant behind pine trees,
Then smile as blood begins its muddy flow,

As yours did, opened to snaked tubes each week
For chemotherapy, which didn't work.
What else was there to do but watch old movies . . .

*

My nappy curls of hair fell to the floor
At your shears' cut. "Nappy"? Friends white
As cirrus clouds, as blinding-clean wordwork,

Or empty appointment slots, which added bite
To moods that swung from stars to thickest mud
Despite the meds and opiated light:

The doors stayed locked, despite the thud
My fists gave for our last scheduled meeting:
"It's this fucking economic crud,"

You'd flung over red wine disappearing
From its box at your last Christmas party . . .

*

Belovèds are the ones we hurt the most,
More than ourselves—bang! a gun, you're toast,
And what will your poor mother think? Lost—

Herself and you in a last breath. Your dad?
We searched address books, but nobody had
A clue. Halfway yours, his Creole blood,

"In the old sense . . ."

*

How could so many talents live as one,
Given our frail flesh: your clouded kidneys
Replaced but with no savior; my sad lungs
Wheezed silver on your easel, the low stars giddy

In an El Greco dusk. Your drawled iambs
And pawn-shop Strat? Fuck *ave atque vale.*

to Jennifer Reeser

Selected Poems

Before the Flood:
A Solo from New Orleans

Crossing Lake Ponchartrain, vertiginous, my hands gripped the wheel,
    And—I'd have sworn it—
The bridge beneath me swayed as a dented maroon Buick passed,
    Radio blaring,
Back seat crammed with children, the Madonna stuck on its dashboard
    Clutching a horseshoe
Of roses. Homelife closing in, I'd scrimped for this day away,
    Not expecting haze,
Heat already swathing the smelly narrow streets, their beer joints

And souvenir shops selling masks half-price after Mardi Gras.
    And not expecting
A clerk's "Don't go past Dauphine, don't go out alone at night" when
    I asked directions.
Wary at noon, I skittered down Bourbon, darting from strippers
    In round-the-clock bars,
Tassels swinging on their siliconed, sweat-beaded breasts, again
    When I saw a man
On his knees at the corner of St. Ann begging for mercy;

The same cry I heard at mass in St. Louis Cathedral, where
    A woman dusk-skinned
As Jeanne Duval sobbed the response, her accent thick as coffee,
    Which I sipped for lunch,
Skimming a secondhand Baudelaire. Such willing confusions
    Of love and disgust:
Ruby-like nipples, syphilis blooming inside her. Hooves clopped
    As a guide retold,
To couples lapsed in his buggy, the history of the convent

And its nuns behind stucco walls—but I'd prayed already, purged
    To bone in shelter
And safety, and now zydeco percussed, delta blues wafted
    Around the statue

In Jackson Square; a young mother balancing a cherub-cheeked,
    Drooling baby dealt
Tarot cards and told my life story so truly I tipped her
    Ten dollars with hands
That shook, then walked smack into two men swapping small envelopes,

Their knife-like stares no match for the Lady of Situations,
    Her stern-eyed blessing
From a card that explained a past, while confirming the future
    Was mine. "When I leave
This town. . . .," but not yet, though the cathedral bell struck its hour;
    I reversed my steps
To sprawl on grass, sniff azaleas, watch a film shoot. Humid skies
    Haloed the city;
A man asked me directions as if I lived there. "When I leave,"

"Cocaine, lady?," "Want a good time, lil' sister?"—if I answered,
    Would I remember
These swells and surges back home, allow them to transform a life
    I can't bid farewell?
And how can we belong anywhere except by peeling shrimp
    And drinking cheap beer
Before divining the way back to our hotels, blurred copies
    Of Baudelaire's poems?
Pigeons' stupid cooing finally woke me; I rushed to make

The check-out time, filling two cracked glasses to rinse my parched mouth
    And throwing matches,
A sweaty nightgown in my duffle. Nearing the bridge, which looked
    More solid, somehow,
Than before, I pulled over, seeing a procession circle
    Raised white tombs then stop,
Jewelling one with flowers, and I joined a woman who opened
    Her throat to echo
And to celebrate loss in that city of flesh and the dead.

Family Battles

1. Christmas 1964

My uncle stares at the TV throughout
Our midday feast, erupts with "Fucking Krauts"
Three times, which I'll repeat on the way home
And be spanked, my Barbie taken from me.
We didn't often see my father's family;
This sad-faced man, introduced as Eddie,
Spent most months at a VA hospital
Thorazined and crying in the chapel
For his buddies, two decades after the invasion
At Ste Mère Église. There seasickness and waves
Wobbled the Allies' legs as bullets kissed
The sand, as mortars spewed from bunkers hidden
Beneath dunes. Eight men from his platoon survived.
Eddie winks at me and twirls the carving knife.

2. Sanctuary / Requiem for a Nun

"St. Mary Magdalene," the rector jokes
As I, dragged to this confirmation class
At dawn, stare dozily through frost-etched windows,
"Is often the girls' favorite . . . " A few blush
At his strange opener; and then I'm passed,
From knees beneath the table, a book one kid
Has filched from home: vein-tangled, sweaty breasts—
Their black bra too—adorn the jacket spread
For Faulkner's tale of Temple Drake. A belle
Turned whore, she's transformed by loss and contrition
When her child dies. ". . . Because hairdressers call
On Mary as"—his chilblained right hand stretched
Toward my bent shag—"their patron slut . . . er, saint."
Free me, O Lord, to burn, or freeze, and pay.

3. Sewanee: 20th College Reunion, 1999

The cornerstone, now thickly choked with weeds
And fallen leaves, is easy to miss—
I scout the path with my flashlight, alert
For snakes. The chapel's bells strike ten; their tower,
Like the black gowns we wore flapping to class,
Pay homage to Oxbridge, which gathered funds
To rebuild a college burned by Union troops:
Those mills belching smoke in Yorkshire landscapes
Would have starved without cheap Dixie cotton.
An antique chest, earrings, some hand-cut glass—
Freed by remains of a maternal dower,
I joined the few girls allowed here, too smart
Not to learn to surrender when amiss
In history class, where home wars rarely bleed.

Witch

Moonlight is infinitely
More dangerous. It sleeps
In the boredom of gray winter nights, dulled
By the flat light of fog.
Only the patient can read.

I have the genius of patience,
Restoring myself to myself, ignoring
The fat croak of distance.
My breath is a shadow for mirrors,
And it holds the whole world.

What can you see there?
A dance of mice, or the slouch
Of great apes? You may wonder, or smile
At your own silhouette:
It's a subject for study,

Like any other, and of as much use
As any other. I am content
As the bird on my shoulder—
My gift to the world, he pecks at,
Hectors the stars.

It's not unfamiliar—they may
Even move. What proof
Do you have against us?
We need no more music, we have
Our own fingers. The smiles of years

Burn in our throats.
The trees are my sentinels,
And they whisper what's near.
I am quite happy here; I like
Being useful.

Bodies

Low-angle shots show Viv, Eliot's hormone-plagued first wife,
Sunk to her knees and scrubbing, scrubbing blood-stained hotel sheets
While her husband walks along the beach, crowded with housewives
And families on holiday. He wishes his new wife
Were like those singing mermaids he wrote poems about in college,
Poems he later recited Camside to court his future wife,
Eyes needy in the flashback as when she becomes his wife,
As when she's pronounced "morally insane," drunk on ether
And raving about thrice-monthly periods and saints. Either
You take his side or you take hers: wives sympathize with wives,
Usually, husbands with husbands, but I fell in love
With Eliot during freshman year, read "Prufrock" and loved

Every last word. Getting pregnant the first time you make love
Is awful luck: my roommate hid in clothes like a fat housewife's,
Spent five months drunk before she finally told her ex-lover
And me, who took the Pill each time I thought I was in love.
A shot and—I'll call her Ruthie—writhed on clinic sheets,
Writhed as I read to her the bedstand's *From Russia with Love*
And *Modern Poets*, read to myself *Saying No and Love*;
And British spies and Prufrock and freak pregnancies collaged
With punk blared from next door, where kids from another college,
In that town we'd come to by bus, heard the death of love
And God and maybe Queen Elizabeth screeched by either
Sid Vicious or Johnny Rotten, or maybe both. "Ether

Is contraindicated for your friend's procedure; ether
Lessens the contractions and the fetus won't expel, love,"
A nurse said on that night's first rounds, the full moon etherous
And clouding over in the windowpane. Smell of ether—
No, Lysol—and Ruthie's sweat. Was Nancy Spungeon a wife,
Or a girlfriend, when her nags sabotaged that haze of ether
Sid wrapped around himself, a heroin drift etherous
And shared like the Chelsea Hotel's cigarette-scarred sheets,
Till he stabbed her dead? I read "Prufrock" aloud, smoothed those sheets,
Fed Ruthie ice chips till she finished screaming in the calm ether
Of the recovery room, dark as that bar near our college
Where the father cried and gave me cash: "Three years of college

And she thought a baby could be wished away?" Back at college,
Ruthie moved to another dorm; by the next year, either
She'd lost contact with me or vice versa, and I left college
For more school, to study those poems Eliot wrote at college
On erotic martyrs like Sebastian and the arrows he loved.
Now Viv dies in the asylum: I'm pulled from friends at college
To recall scenes from that other movie, just after college,
Its scenes razored by Nancy's whine—she was a perfect wife,
If you live in hell and want some company, like a wife.
The two films twine with that clinic, the club's kids from college
Who spewed cheap beer, Ruthie's why not you? muffled by sheets
As I left at twelve to buy cigarettes and stand in sheets

Of rain like tonight's, peering through the door at a torn sheet
Emblazoned with a safety-pinned Queen Liz, at a collage
Of pulsing acrid spotlights, of beer and spit and blood in sheets.
"I'm not an animal," rose Sid's dazed choral leer, sheeting
The words in cutthroat fury. "And I'm not a discharge, either"—
"I'm an abortion." Eliot sent his friend Aiken a sheet
Of the Times once, red-circling words like "mucus," "bloody sheets,"
But this after he'd renounced Viv and her half-mad love.
Aiken's left out of tonight's film, which, like London, I love,
Though I'm travelling alone, sleeping chilled by nylon sheets.
On the late bus, a punk trio—husband, toddler, wife—
Nuzzle each other's spiky hair; he kisses his wife,

Who's given birth to more than rage and pain. Both of us wives
Just after graduation, Ruthie, and I sent you lace sheets
But missed your wedding, write each year in care of the college.
This scrawled postcard will say there aren't any mermaids here, either,
But the punk husband's singing—I swear—a lullaby, with love.

All Those Pretty Ones

A girl's been raped in the snowbound northwest
By six grunge-clad assaulters who crooned Nirvana's
Early hit "Polly": its victim's flowered dress,
The flaring blowtorch & odd pleas for crackers
Are excerpted by the Times, delivered late
In mounting drifts. Quotes from the band's remains,
Though clotted with "you know" & "like," echo Yeats,
Who wondered if his play loosed rage in men
The British shot, if some, like Leda's twins,
Were born to breed terror. Below, wire photos
Of that collapsed zoo aviary in the Bronx,
Nineteenth-century iron staves lying twisted
To ruin, gray-feathered birds pecking at snow.
Where will they fly, cramped wings, indifferent beaks?

The Gold Bird

I fear nothing from winter—
These wings are now gold.
My beak is pure metal,
Open only for song. Mere worms
Cannot hold its attention;
They will thin and grow fickle,
Shrink rootward at autumn's first chill.

Here I practice my high notes
With few interruptions. My old friends
Pass by, and remind me of cold.
They flap their gray wings—
So unkempt and mottled!
Their flight south is mindless,
What really excites them is fish.

Will I miss the young hatchlings,
The sweet trystings by ponds? I'm unsuited
For tropics—I wasted last winter,
Preened my feathers, grew fat.
My soul is at peace here,
And this emperor loves me.
There's no wind in his garden,

It is my song that trembles golden leaves.

Georgia Pilgrimage

Crowds thin as winter nears, as the trees lift
  Their black and twisted limbs toward leaden skies
    That today show no signs of Mary's face.

"Sad but so pretty," said the local farmwife
  Whose sightings drew thousands last summer,
    Church busses unloading the sick and lame,

Those failed by love, in humid air some swore
  Was perfumed with roses. My nose prickles
    At the stale grease that films this diner's booth,

The framed clippings and photos hung above it
  Of a child crowned just last month in a pageant
    When her flaming baton act—I crane to read

Small print—"dropped the crowd to its knees."
  A waitress fills my cup, and, shyly beaming,
    Says she coached her child's routine all year,

Curled the ringlets that halo those pink cheeks.
  They're plump as the cortisone-swollen ones
    Of this state's most famous author, whose face rises,

Her body slumped on crutches, from my book,
  Already sticky but wreathed with coffee-steam
    In this refuge from wind, those now-famed skies

Empty except for leaves. Leaves splotched the road
  That leads back here then to another farm,
    Where Flannery lived with peacocks and her mother,

Whose beatitudes—"pretty is as pretty does"—
  Echo through that story of a crippled girl,
    Acid-tongued and frumpy till she's smitten

With a Bible salesman who steals her wooden leg.
There's enough light to reach the place by sunset,
And the waitress, who took a trip there before

She left high school, bends in a perfumed cloud
And smoothes a spotted menu, drawing a map
To where O'Connor stood at twilight, watched

Her peacocks spread their tails in a strutting pageant
Through the red-clay yard, screeches echoing
Toward each other like electrified applause;

Where she prayed—Mother of God—that her loneliness
Be warmed by more than immaculate beauty,
Those thousand blue and green eyes winking among

Black feathers like stars, beauty that requires
Incense and flowers, prayers that soar sky-high
As it knocks us to unlovely, creaking knees.

Wilde and Pasolini in Heaven

At first, they'll eye each other warily:
Oscar's ruffled cuffs and velvet waistcoat
Seem to scorn, by their Bond Street tailoring,
Pa's tight rayon pants stuffed into cheap boots,
The nylon shirt lurid as Rome's Circus
Or his beloved Pontormos, now displayed
Behind two layers of shatterproof glass.
Gabriel's the go-between, back from forays
To earth, like that garden talk with Mary—
One glance and Oscar's arched brow is levelled,
Pa gulps his jokes about fat British arses
And their queen. Devoted but bickering friends
As years pass: "Each man kills the thing he loves …"
"*Basta*—that sweet punk made tire-ruts my grave."

to David St. John

Independence Day

Charcoal fumes and smolders while my friend piles our plates
    With barbeque, his sauce
A family recipe and praised to the skies. This group's kids
    Soon clamor for ice cream, which we skip to linger
        Over beers in the hot twilight
Circled by mosquitos; when a hand waves one from my neck,
    I mistake the gesture
For my husband's, two chairs away, clasp that hand till someone
    Cracks a joke and I blush,
        Look away so fast I'm dizzied, long-known faces

Suddenly too blurred to connect that one with twins,
    This one with a lost job,
Another with ailing parents. Heat and bugs and voices
    Whirl me from my own place in this humid circle,
        A whirl ridden to distant yards,
Distant blocks—no, ridden farther, till the landscape changes
    And names scatter and dim.
Wasn't our country founded on such dreams of departure,
    Dreams of new arrivals
        Beneath brightly roman-candled skies? That woman

Who's been sleeping for weeks at the mall's parking deck
    Could tell her own version
Over sandwiches and coffee, how her life downspiralled
    From its course of driving carpools and cooking meals,
        The comfort of a husband's touch, most nights.
Could tell how names like "wife" and "mom" were torn from her as
    Quickly as I tear
"Good Samaritan" from myself, who's made her story up—
    I didn't buy dinner
        For this woman and didn't even speak to her

When I fumbled with change among the shadowed cars.
        The sky's now turned jet-black,
And while the toddler twins are sleeping in their mother's arms,
        Their friends fuss and whine, impatient for the fireworks.
        We carry chairs up the yard's slope
To see the spirals and rosettes and fans of tinted light
        Explode through the darkness,
Their patterns widening like the children's mouths, and brighter
        Than Castor and Pollux,
        The Seven Sisters. Oh who's to say that nature

        And history, their unappeasing glut of facts,
        Are children's best teachers,
That even these lines' fantasias won't widen my heart if
        I see the woman at the parking deck again?
        One twin wakes, and reaches toward
The sky's sweet artifice of flare and spark, which remembers
        A freedom-drunk midnight
Long ago in a new world lit mostly by stars, their paths
        Fixed and foretellable
        Until those last blazing gestures toward extinction.

History

It's blood, and generals who were the cause,
Shadows we study for school. In Nashville, lines
Of a Civil War battle are marked, our heroes
The losers. Map clutched in one fist, my bike
Wobbling, I've traced assaults and retreats,
Horns blowing when I stopped. The South's hurried
And richer now; its ranch-house Taras display
Gilt-framed ancestors and silver hidden
When the Yankees came, or bought at garage sales.
History is bunk. But who'd refute that woman
Last night, sashaying toward the bar's exit
In cowboy boots to drawl her proclamation?
"You can write your own epitaph, baby,
I'm outta here—*comprendo?*—I'm history."

Expecting the Barbarians

My table's black marble,
Set for sixteen each night. Maids arrange
The pale linens, my wife cuts the flowers
Herself. She loves blooms
In profusion, I admire the pink throats
Of her lilies, their scent.

And the silver is English, well polished.
It's somebody's heirloom, a family
Of breeding, good taste. The handles
Are plain-cut, they are nothing but edges—
Only women and children need frills.

I indulge my own children, buy them
Fingerpaints, bracelets. My sweet wife is soothed
By gold earrings, details. Our décor's
Her addiction, perhaps too expensive—
The doors here are ebon, gilt-edged.

But I tend to walls, the sparked fences.
The guards are changed nightly and, I suspect,
Well armed. Bright lights
Sweep before them, their straight lines
Assure me. Once or twice
They have wavered, dawn has risen on sidewalks

Splashed and gaudy with blood.

to D.W.

"Whatever You Say, Say Nothing"

No lark, no making light of bombs and kneecappings,
This detour through Derry: according to the map,
A2's the shortest route to the Sligo cottage
Where we've reserved a room. How peaceful it appears
In the glossy brochure's shots: windows wreathed with roses,
And a bay view. Tired, we've just toured Inishowen,

That rock-strewn jut into the Atlantic; no buffer
Between us and the Pole but ocean, we stood in gorse,
The wind stinging my skin, and turned *south* to view Ulster,
An idea so odd you dropped my hand and gouged
Two shapes in sand to explain it. With little coaxing,
I take the wheel, try to adjust the driver's seat,

Glad though half-ashamed of the minor surge of fear
That disperses my travellers' fog. Too much Guinness,
Salt gales and wave-riven shorelines. Our fight last night.
The border crossing's easy, almost a disappointment,
And the city could be any industrial one back home,
Except for its burned-out, windowless rowhouses,

Their bullet-pocked stone walls. Then, on a street whose yards
Are edged with flowers, like our own, soldiers appear:
Cradling rifles, they march in step then pirouette;
Their helmeted, shadowy eyes check left, check right,
What might come at their backs. A routine patrol,
You say, but knock my hand away from the lighter:

Could a lit cigarette look like a threat? The Foyle
Comes into view, and still I put off smoking; the thrill
Of our small dare has dulled, and I'm eager to leave.
Should we have proof, you ask, pointing to roadblocks
Then the backseat, where our loaded camera sits.
The shutter's scarcely closed when guards step from a booth,

Its bulletproof glass sides festooned with razor wire;
People like us just make things worse—I blush, knowing
The soldier right—and he should confiscate our camera,
Arrest the driver. "You must see our side, sir," he says,
Consonants barbed. "We're under terrorist attack here."
You try to shake his hand. He'll let me go this time,

Waving us toward the Republic; "Donegal–Sligo–Leitrim—
The Friendly Counties" have put up a sign as welcome.
Their hills, mist-softened mounds of postcard green, rise
To meet us as Derry's smokestacks become tall smudges
In my rear mirror and radio towers grow distant,
Spikes looped together with wire, dividing the sky.

Blood Oranges

1.

The inn's shuttered against Ávilan noon,
Against a pale, inquisitorial light
That nothing escapes on this windy plain
Where angels swirled into Teresa's dreams,
Such holy dreams her raptured limbs convulsed.
Pain's arrows broke through my habit, and yet,
Receiving this sweetness, my blood sang prayers.
My dreams, less metaphysical, swirl fractured
With parrots clawing at a vendor's cage;
With black-chadored women, arms locked in pairs,
Who duck into boutiques while chauffeurs wait,
Their radios tuned to weirdly wailing pipes;
With Guardía patrols, holsters swung low
By machine pistols. Now the fan's blades waft
My dropped, still-blank postcards, and I want dreams
Of angels too, their wings hymning escape
From travel-smutted flesh, from legacies
Of shuttered rooms and Easter dresses stiff
With starch, the mingled smells of sour milk
And talc—*Those freckles, child!*—as Southern suns
Force dogwoods' buds to cruciforms. At dusk,
My mother and her widowed mother, aunts
Long-widowed too, bless rumors with veiled tones
While I spear carrots, hiding the orange cubes
Beneath my plate. Rumors of their small town's
Adulteries and wayward kids, friends clawed
By sickness—*eaten up, poor soul; they say*
Three months. Clocks chime and my legs twist, stretching
To reach the floor. *God is in the details,*
Teresa said, remembering the arrows,
Those small blood-leaking holes in both her palms.
Above us hang framed oils and photographs,
Their black-gowned women posed against live oaks
Still draped with Spanish moss and razoring

The darkened sky. *God is in the details,*
Said the saint whose corpse smelled of roses
After her death, whose severed hand was carried
Through the countryside *to touch the sick*
And make them whole. To raise the dead.
Though shy, invited to few birthday parties,
I've attended so many funerals,
Dressed in stiff-collared black, that I revise
My bedtime prayer, also terrified I'll die
Before I wake. Everything's inherited here.

2.

Take, for instance, those hummingbirds fluttering
Outside the Toledo farmhouse last week:
Wings zooming up and down, their thin beaks pierced
The cobbled path's geraniums, blooms red
As the birds' throats. Where that path lapsed to dust,
Wind hymned through olive limbs and the sky swirled
With silver-purple clouds, the oily hue
In El Greco's dreamed funeral, its count
And anorexic saints exposed below
Unseen, inhuman hands that leaked lightning.
Two wrong turns in the olive grove, draped with
Low fog that clung to grass and powdery soil,
Wet my legs to the knees; and I startled
A hare, frozen in the dawn chill as steam
Puffed from both our nostrils. *No blessings here,*
The wind translated, except for those who watch
The sun rise till the ground scorches and ask
For still more heat, for those who reach to stroke
That quivery fur, who seek delight in gorse
And trampled poppies, that tail's uplifted flash.
Jet-lagged and lost in the dense-misted grove,
A near-hallucination of scrawny trunks

With dusty, blade-shaped leaves, I stopped, wheezing,
To search for my inhaler, felt my heart claw
Its narrow cage of countably stark ribs
Till noises from the farmhouse—kettle-shrieks,
Pots banged against a sink—told me which way
Was home. For a day. I travel to make peace
With mine till I'm exhausted with strangeness,
With washing shirts in rust-streaked bathroom sinks
And the black aftertaste of bitter coffee,
With sneezing fits mimed nightly for housemaids—
Habla inglés?—who bring more feather pillows
And stare like stones. The cobbled path grown hot
Beneath their crimson throats, the blurry wings
As darkly translucent as mourning veils,
The hummingbirds hurt each other away
From those blossoms with rapier beaks, also
Their tiny claws. But sharing doles of grace,
Small bits of heaven's dust drifted to earth,
Is unknown in the animal kingdom
As in childhood's domain: *you touch my blocks,*
My dolls, my collection of butterflies,
And I'll tell, I'll smash what you love, I'll kill you.

3.

For Lorca, flight to Andalusía
Brought neither lost youth back nor shelter from
The war, but only bullets splintering
The dust-veiled olive trees—whose childhood blessings
Were more bloodily mixed? On the dawn train,
I lapsed from views of his sun-fractured landscape
To a nap's dreams swirled by his aunt, reborn
As the black-habited Bernarda Alba,
Who shuttered her windows against the sun
And stars, who insisted her girls die virgins.

Her homely scepter's law knocks even here:
Streets jammed with late diners, with kids who spill
From Madrid's pulsing clubs to jostle those
Still hawking Marvel comics or mantillas.
Or toy machine pistols. Or rabbits' feet.
Or the next booth's drag-sized black lingerie,
Which two skateboarder boys poke sneeringly.
Their words aren't in my phrasebook, but recalled
From Lorca's gorgeous, self-hating tirade
Against Manhattan's sidewalk queens: *cancos,*
Maricas. Back at home, we drawl the name
Of our own *Andalooo-shha,* a town near where
En Sangre Fría's author, his cherub's face
Still pretty on the next booth's paperbacks,
Was raised by aunts who called him *sissy-britches.*
Later, he felt more at home with murder
Than small-town Southern life, despite a love
For its landscape, the oaks silvered with heat
And hanging moss that draped my early dreams
Of heaven. Some find it on earth, he wrote,
In windows filled by jewel-stained light, a light
Suffusing grace through cities yet unknown.
Miss Holiday Golightly. Dead Lorca fell
Beneath smoke-pluming guns; Tru's last book bore
Teresa's words about unanswered prayers.
What do they share, and I with them, beyond
A language of desire and shame, of homes
Escaped then mourned? Andalusian oranges—
I buy a bag, their scent acidly sweet
Through waxed paper, sweet as envisioned love
Made real. Why travel except this desire
For linkage, even skewed; its fruits blessings
We've dreamed foreign, their varied tastes received
And welcome as this blood orange leaking its sting
Down my square, freckled, inherited chin?

Reunion Banquet, Class of '79

"What happened to Charlotte Rampling?"—the vamp
And villainess of freshman year's remake,
Farewell, My Lovely. I can't recall the plot,
Nor which boyfriend I went to see it with,

None villains. Freshman year, girls learn to drink;
We spent weekends bombed in years that followed,
Often with this old boyfriends, some seated
In nearby chairs as we discussed *Three Women, Klute*

("Poor Sutherland—what was the bomb that followed?"
"Fellini's *Casanova*"); Jane Fonda
Changing women from fat dateless klutzes
To lean wives, marrying "that Turner guy,

A fellow Casanova before Jane."
Chinatown, Looking for Mr. Goodbar,
Diane Keaton ferrying from guy to guy,
Then killed. *Helter Skelter*, a TV movie

Looked at with Chinese food and tepid beer,
That crammed dorm room (soph year? junior?) our knees
Jellied. Hell, what's better than the movies
For filling gaps, for steering talk away

From this crammed corner's melodramas, its queens
Of bad luck? Emma's three miscarriages—
"Children fill a gap"; talk tries to veer away
But she tells us about her absent husband,

Who blames their bad luck on her mom's DES,
How she spends Saturday nights now, fevered
By secrets she doesn't tell her husband:
Chlamydia and one nostril scarred from coke,

For instance. *Saturday Night Fever!*
Someone yelps, and Nan's atop the table—
Clam sauce spotting her skirt, a Diet Coke
Spilled—in the famous John Travolta pose;

Someone yelps as Nan tips from the table,
As Layne prescribes a single mom's sanity:
Sitcom repeats, like the John Travolta show
About the teacher, while she plugs into

Tapes that prescribes ways to keep your sanity
While raising a small boy alone. Virginia
Weeps—loudly—about the teacher who plugged her
Senior year, and the men at the next table

Rise to leave. "So long, boys," and "virgins,"
Sneers Laura, meaning none have been divorced,
Not since senior year, when one at their table
Tied the knot and wanted out weeks later.

The Deer Hunter. Most seated here are divorced,
And childless too. Lipstick. *Who'll Stop the Rain?*
I untie my knotted napkin, wanting out. It's late.
A Woman Under the Influence. Badlands.

"What happened to our apple charlottes?" Vanished,
Like our lipsticked smiles, the bottles of wine.
We're women fluent with address pads and pens:
Farewell, my lovelies. "I'll call, or write."

The Storm

Why shouldn't I stay, whispered part of myself—
He'd stocked plenty of groceries for three,
Maybe four days. Red wine too, a whole case.
The ice, like a bright skin, had covered the trees
And main road to the nearest town. A wreck,
The car crashed, was what I imagined—there
Were things I feared more than adulterous sex.
And he'd touched me already, kissed my hair
And chapped lips: how much further could I fall?
Winds howled an old answer and I thought of
Francesca, swirling in that second circle.
Life wasn't bad, for hell. Whispering *love*—
But not just for one night—through those great gusts
Of wind, God, shouldn't she have been pleased?

Gauguin in Alaska

I long for an orange, the sharp bite
Of citrus. Something sun-warmed,
And knowing south air.
My teeth here soften on blubber.

The fur-wrapped women squint and blink
In cold sun. They are no comfort,
Smelling of whale fat, the oiled odor
Of smoke. They thicken

On nine months' winter.
And I dislike the strange light—
Nothing is blurred. All is too sharp,
Ice-edged.

Sometimes s serpent uncoils in night air.
He tempts me to nothing.
I watch him glitter, blind in his sky—
Such shimmer is empty, frost-born.

There's no lover's light here, no sea
I can sleep by, no roar but the flat howl
Of wind. The women are frightened,
They say he is hungry.

The men are out hunting, they have taken
Their spears. The women also
Are hungry. They worry me, huddled together
At night, all giggles and blankets.

I do not trust them.
One has taken my brushes, thinking them magic.
She offers stiff bristles
Of hair.

i. m. S.H.

78

The Last Violet

Mary Jane Kelly, 1863-1888

1.

Limerick, sir? *Sweet flows the River Shanno*n,
Or don't you know that song? I spent girlhood
In neighborhoods more posh than Whitechapel,
Its butcherhouses' stink and rummies slumped
By Maiden Lane, where some woo rougher trade
Then shrink beneath a sweaty fist in rooms
Like this: *o murder's* heard here late at night
Almost as often as St. Mary's bells,
The same cry heard when Jack still wore nappies.
'Tis a comedown for me, raised to paint china,
Embroider silk and linen, taught to sing—
Only a violet's my favorite—
By mam before she and the last babe died.
My first stop here in London was the same
As all good Irish girls', some glad to scrub
A convent's floors for porridge and a cot,
But who'd call these fair wages? Even here—
Ma maisonette—I keep a lady's ways:
This basin, my bottle of French perfume
And that small one of brandy—there, a nip
Will take the chill November from your bones.
Thieves stole my oil lamp and the wee portrait
By Walter Sickert, no less, when I took ill
With quinsy, fevered in that infirmary bed.
Now I sleep days after twisting the sheets
With proper husbands in derbies like yours—
Lord's name, are you really a bachelor?—
Who go home late to their wives, long asleep,
Milk-faced and tight-kneed, dreaming of the Queen.

2.

That courtship teaches whoring's mortal shame
But true: young girls trade kisses for bouquets,
Let sweaty hands roam their breasts in return
For tuppence frills and bows. *Only a violet . . .*
I'd fancied marriage more romantic than
A ring and overnight at Cardiff, Davies'
Sod-drunk sleeps soon as he got the mine's pay
And fun from me. E'er dirty, he'd roll off
To snore, and, turning up the lamp, I'd check
For smudges—you, like true gents, look to know
That soap and water won't melt bones. Davies
Died in the explosion that also killed
The dads, who'd dragged us all cross-channel when
Sacked from the Limerick bank: barely nineteen
I was, and left to scrimp for London fare;
Then how I cursed the dads, cursed how he'd drained
My dowry soon as we'd shut poor mam's eyes
With coppers. Roaring he'd be, and gutter-mouthed
At table; my greasy brothers smirked, the lot,
When he'd thunder there was one place besides
The kitchen where a woman was good company.
Only a violet . . . sacking, threats
From the landlord, and sending off Brigid,
Whom mam had hired as maid, her cheeks still raw
From Galway winds—she'd blush crimson and drop
Her eyes to the joint when dads was four sheets,
Blush and wait for him to stop laughing at
His own blather and start carving the meat.

3.

The West End house? Two dozen oil lamps dripped
With silk fringe, lovey; bare feet disappeared
Into plush Persian rugs. The men there were
The lot's best, so well-mannered they'd say "sorry"
For coming. You like a good laugh, don't you?
One gent hired me for a full week in Paris,
Six giddy nights with oysters and champagne,
A feather bed. That poor dim James, a fiend
For culture, plucked my elbow in the Louvre—
"Coo now! What you call that?"—and exclaimed loud
By stained church windows, checking his moustache
In Notre Dame's carved font. Its statue of
The Virgin, my name-saint, gave me the shivers;

Though one Sunday when James was still asleep
I skittered in before the eight o'clock
To light a candle for that wee sister
I never held, for mam, even one for
The dads. *Hail Mary, full of grace, blessèd*
Art thou among women and blessèd is . . .
A priest two rows away looked up from prayers
Like I'd raved curses; he startled and made
The cross's sign with his smudged, crookèd fingers
Then backed, black-frocked, through an open door.

4.

"Black Mary," jealous wenches nicknamed me
At the Ten Bells . . . less elegant—or *luxe*—
Than the West End house, but nobody takes
A cut, and I've now regulars who queue
For more than evening pints. *Marie Jeannette,*
I whisper when I miss those nights beside
The Seine; once, the slut most covetous
Heard and began to screech like the banshee—
"Her real name's Mary Jane! 'Black Mary' Jane!"
So loud she screeched, my fellow spilled his ale . . .
Pour us a bit more brandy, there's a love.
I don't deserve "Black Mary," I tell myself
When I look into mirrors, my hair flax-blond
And smile sweet as a girl's, plump as those days
I posed for Walt Sickert; I don't deserve
These filthy walls, no matter what I call them,
Nor deserve waking at dusk to find grey rats
Worrying my naked feet. When in her cups,
My friend Liz brogues away about the kirk
And its free destinations . . . "Mary, Marie,
Are you listening to me, lass?" I'll have none
Of a Scot's destinations, I say straight,
But her head bows as she claims the parson
Meant that we're doomed to certain things by God—
"Like our monthlies," she moans. The only time
I'm black-tempered. After, I'm back fluttering
My lashes and silk fan, and with bells on.

5.

A suspect's jailed, but Fleet Street ragmen buzz
Like flies to fresher blood: Queen Vicky's eighth
And chloroformed lie-in a scandal to some:
Is it not women's curse to bring forth babes
In pain? Abortionists sell laudanum,
Which I'd drink every night if my labors
Paid more; now even brandy's seeming dear,
My regulars afraid of Whitechapel,
Afraid old Jack might rip them too! 'Tis kind,
Indeed, for you to walk me from the Bells,
To praise my voice: *Only a violet*
Plucked from my mother's grave—och, the neighbors
Complain at any wee noise, make more fuss
Than alley cats, or that pate-addled drunk
Who's whingeing chorus . . . The halfpenny candle
Gutters, but lately I've not dared close my eyes
Till the dawn breaks, and still, I suffer dreams—
Your derby might hang there, love, near the bag
And gloves—dreams of that murderous blade yellowed
By candlelight and plunging for my throat,
More like one of Sickert's paintings than real;
And in the worst I bowed to hell's own steel,
Just like back home in Limerick I bowed
To the cross our priest hefted, my head dipped
Ready and willing, belly shrunk from fasts,
Shake-kneed and cunt nun-dry . . . be a good heart
And fetch the quilt. I'd steal peeks at the statue
Of Jesus, the red sword-gash in his side,
Those slender, near-girly legs ankle-crossed
Below blood mingled with pale curls and thorns.

i. m. Anthony Hecht

Chorale

A sack of rotting apples dizzied Schiller's brain
As he wrote, drunk on scent
And words, those now-unread plays, even *Wilhelm Tell* recalled
Only for its hero, whose arrows sang through air
To find their red, heart-shaped targets.
My friend fills her syringe while I search for my car keys, turn
to see the needle plunged
into her left thigh: "diabetes," she tells me

en route to the café, means "siphon," the body
melting down to water;
"mellitus" describes the sweet smell of the patient's urine.
Pouring vials near an anthill was the ancient test
For this disease; if the ants swarmed,
The prognosis was coma, followed by that deepest sleep,
Sugar levels risen
So high they thrum the blood to stasis. In August,

When her lover went back home to his wife, my friend
Skipped one shot, two, skipped meals
To binge on twelve-hour naps, waking to nibble candy
And hear, through the thin walls, an elderly neighbor
Playing sonatas. "Ode to Joy,"
Schiller's most famous work, though we nearly lose the lyric
In Beethoven's grand chords,
The 9th Symphony composed after his ears closed

To all but music, as my friend's eyes closed to all
But the black-winged angel.
That neighbor heard no footsteps or rattle of plates for days,
Worried enough to call and ask if I had keys:
Even outside the dark bedroom
We smelled the perfume of—roses? No, fruity and cloying,
Like a sack of apples
Left to rot. The ambulance crew filled a syringe

On arrival, trained for signs of blood sugar soared
  Sky-high. "Dumb thing to do,"
My friend says, scanning the menu and sipping Diet Coke,
  And I'm not sure if she means the man or her try
    At self-destruction, drowning
In a forbidden rapture. The last time I fell in love
    I played Beethoven
  So loud that pictures trembled and china rattled

  Its shelves, *Chorale*'s strings and winds and horns confirming
    That joy—*Freude, Freude*—
Is what we all desire, that while deep-kindled by the scent
  Of hair, or the brief feathery touch of a hand,
    Of the sight of a parted mouth,
Desire arrows its way into the brain till flesh and mind
    Become as one, singing
  Our unrequitable ache to drown in sweetness.

The Dolls

Those lolling china heads and rag-stuffed arms
Will never love us in return, said Rilke,
Whose mother dressed him like a girl, whose charms

Were sealed in letters for his distant harem.
"How dreadful," he wrote, "to spin our first silk"
For lolling china heads, for rag-stuffed arms

As plump as mine when young, the rich aroma
Of cakes rising, cream rising in whole milk.
My mother dressed me like a girl who'd charm

Her grown-up friends at teas, stroll through museums
And fall in love with statues, like Rilke,
Those lolling china heads and rag-stuffed arms

Turned to marble Apollos in his poems:
"Change your life." Easy for a god to talk—
No mother dressed him like a girl whose charms

Were pink and minor, who blinked with alarm
Whenever boys asked if she loved them back.
O lolling china heads and rag-stuffed arms—
Still I undressed, a girl with other charms.

to Richard Howard

The Triumph of Style

A blond goddess at ninety, unrivalled now that Dietrich's dead,
  Her spotted hands clutch
A cane, though her legs—stockingless, blue-veined—look sturdy enough,
  Their hard roped muscles
Testifying to the German love for fresh air, pine forests
  With thick-needled floors
Right out of Hansel and Gretel, the world of *Lederhosen*,

Lebensraum. She feels betrayed still, this glossy magazine says,
  By the investors
Who snapped their purses shut after a pistol kissed Hitler's throat,
  After Berlin fell
In a mangle of smoking concrete, after Auschwitz, Belsen,
  Dachau, that litany.
Now still shoots are her forte: these Nuba tribesmen—some pluming spears,

Others dressing a lion's carcass—could be dark-skinned versions
  Of Aryan youth,
Muscular and schooled to conquer worlds, breed with lithe blond women,
  To ponder Wagner
While snow swirls outside, shattered from gables in red-tinted dawns.
  All's shattered tonight
In Miami, after a hurricane's spin through that city

Of slums and sugar-grained beaches, sky-high murder rates, Disney
  And the purest coke
North of Bogotá. Keening winds silenced murmurs from doorways
  Offering dreams that last
Through the next pipe, for the youthful gold chains and teeth, tennis shoes
  At two hundred bucks
A pop. Who blames their hoisting white flags on adolescence's

Battleground, their looks from mirrors to store displays, wanting to
  Be *wicked gorgeous*,
Wanting to lavish a project's tiny closet with leather
  And silk, to be famed

For having *style*? The *Times* photographer, his lenses trained on
    Destruction's glamour,
Took the picture that caught my notice fastest: a mannequin,

Eyes thick-lashed, blown from a beachside Saks window, her wigless head
    Resting on pavement
While her pelvis held its thrust-out pose, arms still cocked and attached
    To bone-sharpened hips.
Leni's camera cocked upward, in its most notorious image,
    To heighten a man
Small above those Nuremberg crowds, stiff-armed and -legged with salute,

His platform's marble lions like Pergamon's. Thousands of mouths roared
    Führer, swelling winds
That blew for six years. We mouth platitudes on nature and force,
    Turn up our noses
At Jeffers' adoring tales of vultures and murderous cliffs,
    But style's a force too,
As Riefenstahl herself would tell you, or the armed ten-year-old

Found looting a Gap store among hissing electrical wires
    And fallen palms, or
This mannequin, whose grainy portrait I've taped above my desk,
    Her vatic silence
Somehow louder than gales on TV, and full of the meaning
    Given ornament,
The cruel myth held inside those blind, mascaraed, staring eyes.

Bringing Home the Bacon

*"Nowadays, it's often the husband who rings
us up to see if we'll take his wife on."*

—manager of a strippers' agency in Tyneside, England

His father sleeps full-clothed downstairs.
Yet I'm wanting no company—I go to my son's room,
Smell his child's sweat, from games.
He turns when I kiss him, a small snorer already.

The telly's still on, and these nights
I'm glad. I spend pounds on hot baths,
Have bought perfumes and oils, a new bathrobe
And gowns. (These are practical things,

I picked them both strictly for warmth.)
I've my eye on fur coats, and I feel I've a right—
I can't work if I'm sickly, perhaps in two years
I'll have mine. Yet the telly's now ours—

I bought it, it's paid for. And the wee one
Has toys, he smiled all Christmas Day.
My own sits with telly, he takes his drinks
At home—he gives his son no mind at all.

With the lot of them neighbors, it seems
In good fun. They're out of jobs too—
It's hard to point blame. They wave pints;
I'm cheered at least three times a show.

I don't mind it much, except for the cold.

Matinées

1. PeeWee's Big Adventure, 1993

The theater's dark. Onscreen, a couple sweats,
Limbs twined crazily atop a bed that looks
Loaned from the Playhouse: scattered bright pillows float
Like huge gumdrops above the sheets, unfocused
And milky. Paulie, as his mother calls him,
Curls in the row's last seat, his long hair wet
With Palm Beach rain, cheeks unpowdered, lips thin
And parting. Too original for raincoats,
He wears jeans and a Barney T-shirt washed
Soft as a child's pajamas. Which she's kept.
With baby teeth, report cards, and a stash
Of clippings to bring out for company:
Him. Twice yearly. Now a flashlight points down,
Cutting the aisle. The cop isn't clowning around.

2. Pretty Babies: Malle Festival, 2000

In her first film, Brooke Shields is barely twelve,
The same age as Violet, the Storyville whore
Whose cherry's sold to the highest bidder:
She lowers that swath of crimson velvet
To pose on a pedestal, waving sparklers.
Now Bellocq positions mother and daughter
On a loveseat's plush, tugs at one's camisole,
The other's pantalettes, wanting symmetry:
Black neck-ribbons, black hose rolled to the knee
Make the two look like sisters, one slightly older.
Brooke will grow rich modelling designer jeans,
Mrs. Shields permit other, longer nude scenes.
Bellocq adjusts the lens. Pretty Mama glows.
Reader, hush your mouth. This is the world she knows.

i. m. Jerry Wexler

Bad Blood

A woman stares, wild-eyed from the terror known only when death,
    That black-winged angel,
Appears without warning, without any time for prayers, rescue,
    Or bargains; appears
In a speeding car, in a plane plummeting a thousand feet
    Per second; appears
As a murderer's knife, unsheathed and glittering. Her wet blond hair,

Grayish in the black-and-white film, drips at the sides of her face
    And emphasizes
Those eyes, that darkly lipsticked mouth shaped in a scream's darker *o*.
    Blood spatters the tile
Then the cracked drain, its perforations swirling with stained water.
    Flashbacks to *Psycho*:
What middle-ager doesn't succumb, at least in motel showers;

Or recall the last shots, of Bates tied down while a fly roams
    His twitching fingers?
A man too gentle to hurt a fly, the voice-over repeats.
    With brute surrender,
The actor embodied our worst fears—like dying in the bath,
    When we're defenseless,
Trusting water like a lover to soothe, to cleanse off the grit

And smudges of ill-spent pasts, to give us new starts. No new start
    For a man offered
Only crazed killer roles in his short life, who quoted a film
    In his dying days.
An easier story: everyone knew Germans were the bad guys,
    That Ingrid Bergman's
Suffering was noble, though her career was nearly sunk by . . .

Living in sin? Out-of-wedlock kids? One era's moral rage
    Is lost as quickly
As the next shapes its fears. *Keep me safe, keep me safe*—we repeat
    Craven litanies now,

In time of plague, want to feel singled out and cherished by God,
    Who'll surely spare us,
Our friends, our families. Almost sensual, these open-mouthed pleas

For blessing, as when we let water sluice its warm passage down
    Our flesh at the end
Of a day that's pummeled us into exhaustion and blankness,
    When we drop our hands
To unbutton a shirt, pull on the iron teeth of a zipper,
    Look in someone's eyes
And pray *Love me, treasure my body, don't ever let me die.*

Story Hour

Near the parking lot, a few last red leaves swirl—
Catch me, catch me if you can—toward twilit skies
Scarred with late autumn's frozen bits of cirrus.
Or are they contrails? A jet's roar lifts my eyes—

Catch me, catch me if you can—toward twilit skies
And I walk too close to a kid-crammed car,
Which swerves and tailspins. Snow White lifted her eyes,
Still drugged with sleep, for a smitten prince;

But walking too close to a kid-crammed car,
My eyes updrifting with those red swirled leaves,
Is dangerous. Like sleeping with a smitten prince—
But that's a fairy tale. Here's a true story,

One that little kids, driven home through leaves
From neighborhood libraries, shouldn't hear—
It's a scary tale—though this true story
Ends with justice done: last night at a bar

Near the library, my friend said she'd just heard
That the man who's raped ten local woman
Had been arrested, been locked behind bars.
Married, a father of twins, he lives nearby,

This man who's raped ten local woman
(I've seen him around, mowing his backyard
Or tossing balls for kids who live nearby);
He's described and named by the newspaper

I found this morning in our frost-flecked yard,
The glass like crystal. My friend talked of his wife,
Also described and named in the newspaper,
Then sipped her red wine. "She'll never be the same."

We looked at men and talked of being wives,
And lipstick, but kept other secrets. Last week
A man I can't forget said he felt the same,
Looking at me in this library parking lot

(I've kept secret about this since last week)
As he did when looking at old pictures
Of his ex, who'd worked at the library
And lived with him but without warning moved

To Colorado, which she'd looked at in pictures.
My friend, an alarmist, once said rapists
Often stalk victims at libraries or movies.
But in this parking lot, that man's eyes shone lonely,

And I've walked back here every day. A rapist,
Or a prince, who might return with a kiss?
This empty parking lot now shines lonely
With the half-swallowed sun, cars bound for home.

Should I hope he'll return with a kiss,
Having trailed me here? A jet's roar lifts my eyes.
I'm wearing red lipstick, which I don't at home.
Catch me, catch me if you can, beneath twilit skies.

Foucault in Vermont or Antonioni????

No author for this fall landscape, nor signs
Of limits tested, except the fence just yards
From I-89, and a stray Holstein
Unfazed by traffic headed for the border.
How different from your time in California,
Those LSD trips at Zabriskie Point,
Warm nights spent cruising, or in Castro's bars
With studded whips and chains, implements
Not of love but knowledge: "to find God—
Or truth—in moments when the greatest pain
And pleasure are melted into one." De Sade
And de Chardin. The virus swarms your brain . . .
But now this woolen hat. No melting here,
A state fist-fucked by winter every year.

Duplex Noir

At dusk, stars fizzle in this landlocked sky
And TV screens turn blue, like smoke rising
From my neighbors' grill, smoke perfumed with meat
And already-spilled booze (they've brought enough):
Bourbon for backslapping men, gin and tonic
For those first dates, white wine for moms who call

Their sitters every hour. You haven't called;
My set darkens with Florida night sky,
Hurt and Turner sweating over tonics
Slopped with rum, the tang of cut limes rising
As they plot to kill her husband. Enough—
I've seen Body Heat twice before, Matty

And Ned scheming to make Richard Crenna meat,
Dead burned meat, between drinks and fucks and calls
Dialed from pay phones. I've never had enough
Of Florida, seared breeze and mackerel skies
At sundown, my sand-crusted knees rising
From castles left to watery tectonics

As my parents, gins lightly splashed with tonic,
Picked at olives, cheese, cold sliced meats
And sang my name, their slurred voices rising
Like the waves. Channel Eight: Lauren Bacall
In Martinique, monochromatic skies
And rum-runner Bogart, who's had enough

Of Vichy thugs, who's never been loved enough,
As any dame can see. The movies are tonic
But addictive for little girls too shy
To play with boys, who cry into their meat
At dinners years later, when boys don't call
And when they do, when her father's shouts rise
And shake her bedroom walls. The volume rises
Next door where they've had more than enough,

The married and the single both. One call—
That's all it would take, and what's more tonic
Than flesh on flesh. I could arrange to meet
You anytime. Stars vibrate in the sky,

Now black above rising wires, trays of tonic
And leftover booze: they've burned enough meat
To call for pizza. Late news. No choice of skies.

92 Johnson Avenue, 1985

"Women, women, the whole house stank of them,"
Plath wrote in girlhood journals; I've mapped a drive
Through Wellesley streets reddened by fallen leaves
To find where she'd lived with Aurelia, dreamed
Of Daddy rising from Azalea Path,
Coming back to buy her pretty dresses.
Betrayed again, she honed words into scythes
That still draw blood: grayed Hughes arrives in Boston
The next month for a lawsuit; called "Murderer"
By those protesters frothing with old rage,
He's so handsome on TV my knees water.
"Take us away from here," two daughters sang
In white suburban houses, dads absent,
Hoping to lure princes, sex our gaudy bait.

i.m. F. X. Toole

Descant

Beneath the sidewalk's iron gates, those ice-slicked portals
    To an underworld of trains
  Whose tunnelled rush became a woman's voice—
How easy, in that long Manhattan winter, to hear Persephone
    Mourning sunlit earth and its maternal warmth,
      Also mourning the taste
    Of those sweet red seeds. How easy now to hear
      Her whisper through chill wind,
    A thousand miles south from a man who whispered love

    Deep in his throat as snow-pocked obsidian windows
      Turned violet then crimson.
  Beyond my empty classroom's rattling panes,
A tree clings to its few last gaudy leaves; from the parking lot
    Of this girls' school, some muted rock and roll rises
      With forbidden smoke.
  Who wants to study when her winter prom
      Is just a week away?
    By then more letters will crowd my gradebook's pages

    In a well-ordered train. But what chaotic gods
      The heart has always worshipped,
    And would my students gape in disbelief
If I told them how quickly I undress when someone whispers love,
    Shed my clothes on floors that seem to cleave
      Beneath my feet? Outside,
    Those almost-naked trees surround a fountain
      Like the mythic one
    That virgin goddess vanished by; its chitoned girls

    Shyly bend their heads as Cupid grins and clutches
      His bow, graffiti scrawled
  On one plump leg: *Virginia* ♥ *Harry*.
Aren't all women Persephone, lost to the dark allure of sex
    Between parted sheets, waiting for flesh to warm them
      While invisible mothers

Tear their long robes, cry to the chilling earth
  And cloudy deaf heaven?
  Clasping that man's body, once I whispered the name

  Of a daughter as longed-for, and even untouched,
    As the body mourned
By any woman who's lost herself again,
A daughter whose first sounds would silence the parking lot's traffic
    And rustling trees outside, a daughter like me
    Whose cry said *I'll love you*
Till trees turn red with fruit and dying leaves,
    Till your sweet eyes are closed
  With pennies; I'll leave you for love for love for love.

Hurricane Walk

It was better than sex, the way it relaxed me.
My thighs throbbed for hours, each finger
Seemed limp. I lighted
A cigarette, then found it too heavy to lift.

A more comfortable lust would have kept me
Inside. Yet I wanted
The wind's touch, to feel its whorled force.
I stood on a bridge, there were no trees

To stop it—I saw thin sheets of water
Spin like ghosts from the Charles.
And now, damp from a bath, I feel
Honed, quite essential.

This robe seems too big, it abrades
My cleansed skin. The room's warmth
Stings my lips; they were left raw and chapped,
Almost bruised. It will take days

To heal them, the slightest good-night kiss
Is out of the question for weeks.

Home Thoughts from Abroad

1. *Reunions: Kensington, 2004*

Jet-lagged, yanking my mother's huge suitcase
Like a leashed and mutant dog, I stumble
Through the jammed lobby, a chill morning haze
Sooting the V & A's imperious walls
Beyond a bank of windows. "We're headquarters,"
The clerk explains politely when I ask
Who all those loud gray-haired Americans are,
"For the 82nd Airborne." First I'm blank,
Then alarmed—war again, and this one fought
By those nearing death, as Rousseau suggested,
Our hotel commandeered for drills and cots?
"Their reunion," the clerk adds, and how stupid
To forget D-Day's 60th, how vets
Would come in swarms. No rooms are ready yet.

2. *Announcements: Jackson Boulevard, 1967 and 1980*

"I hate babies—they mess up your nice things,"
My mother shrieks, my brother spitting up
On her bed's counterpane, hand-tatted lace.
And like her china, even her wedding ring,
Among the last heirlooms long ago shipped
From a parent country that preferred nannies
And marriage for bloodlines, not happiness.
My mother's was "beneath her, a disgrace,"
Said a great-aunt once, half-drunk on sherry.
How long before their unblessed love turned bitter?
Rigid beneath blankets, I pray that they'll divorce
Through years of long wall-trembling arguments.
The night I tell my mother I'm engaged,
She cries, of course, and offers me her ring.

3. *Half-Day Bus Tour: London, 2004*

Our guide has told the joke a thousand times,
Sir Winston's drunk retort to Lady Astor,
Her ugly forwardness a female crime
In any century. "Victoria,"
He points to a monument, "dressed in black
For forty years to mourn Prince Albert's death."
Next a story about Brits' love for pets,
But I'm tuned out, my attention distracted
By London's dusk-lit glow, till the punchline,
Something about wives and dogs, all bitches.
My husband's trampling down the Yorkshire Dales;
What stories does he tell to gain strangers' smiles
There, opting for hikes, not museum riches?
Here the loot of a hearthbound queen's empire.

4. *Steward of the Signet Society: Boston, 1985*

"Larkin's dead!" The escutcheoned door slams hard
Behind an undergrad who's six months late
With dues; his friends at the lunch table
Drop their silver forks, slosh tears and sherry
On the linen cloth I'll later have to wash
And iron. Fourteen grand a year, plus free rent
Right in Harvard Square—how could my husband,
A broke midlife 2L, and I refuse?
Modelled on Oxbridge literary clubs,
The Signet has a library, small bar,
Members who've perfected British phrasing—
"White coffee," "bonking her"—but that day flub
Quoting those poems that comprehend the heart,
How it craves love, also deprivation.

5. *Portobello Road, 2004*

How I loathe shopping, especially in crowds,
My backpack so loaded with Mother's finds—
Tea caddies, butlers' trays—I nearly waddle
To the next stall; she fingers christening gowns,
Then, stricken by her childless daughter's wince,
Seizes on a gift of silver earrings.
"Victorian," the dealer swears, then bows,
And points to what he calls his china darlings,
A row of dolls so cloyingly sweet-faced
They're icons for this country's child-worship,
Still reeling from that gruesome railyard case:
Three boys, two murderous, their four hands gripped
On film. A quick parole, adoption offers.
Let them rot, I say. Weep for their mothers.

6. *Jackson Boulevard, 1972, and Fitzroy Road, 1963*

Both houses white, both haunted by Furies
Who took their revenge as good women do,
Not with guns or knives but black depressions,
One's hair falling lankly from an oven door
As hissing gas choked out her eulogy;
The other crying in bed through whole seasons,
Wearing the same nightgown as summer air
Sharpens into fall, as I learn Shakespeare
And history, also how to clean a house,
Make dinners for my brother and my father,
When he's not travelling; how to wash
And iron between problems for geometry.
My favorite book in high school? *The Bell Jar.*
Recurring nightmare? Sheets stained, her wrists slashed.

7. Tom and Viv: Jackson Boulevard, 1973, and Piccadilly Cinema, 2004

"To be moral, I suppose"—here Dafoe,
Who plays Eliot, looks upward from the rug
As though God dwelt within the chandelier—
"One must first be damned." The film gets better,
But the marriage can't survive Viv's bloody rags,
Head-blurring pills quacks said would stanch the flow
That continued red for weeks. She sniffed ether
And gave her husband his best Cockney lines:
What you get married for if you don't want
Children? At sixteen I knew what I wanted:
To be Prufrock, remote from those women,
Pliant and perfumed, whose arms were downed with hair;
To write poems singing as Eliot's dry bones—
Viv, a faithful wife, died in an asylum.

8. Westminster Abbey, 2004

Just a few minutes until evensong:
Poets' Corner closed, I buy a brass rubbing
Of Shakespeare, whose remains lie undisturbed
Elsewhere, if grave robbers still fear curses,
The anger of the dead come home to roost.
Head bowed over packages, the hard pew
Surely spasming her back, my mother
Doesn't move as the black-robed junior choir
Processes. How tired she looks, and worn,
As I slip in beside her; the loft's organ
Sounds "Love Divine, All Loves Excelling," which soars
Above the cracking voice of one young tenor.
She pats my hand, smiling; God, what forms can
Love take except the smudged, the failed, the human?

9. The Tower, 1986 and 2004

The Thames whitecapped: wind stands our hair on end,
Drowns out the Yeoman's spiel and the clamor
Of ravens we're warned not to touch: they bite,
Perhaps exacting payment for those clipped wings,
Which ensure they'll stay put and the Tower
Never fall, still faithful to the legend.
My husband, who brought me here on a past visit,
This year wanted our vacations kept separate,
His treks remote. The Yeoman defends Richard,
A hunchback but no killer: "cripples were feared"—
Mother and I bend under low ceilings—
"Being thought to bear the mark of Satan."
Some marks don't show. The crippled heart resists
The world—but how sick I am of prisons.

10. St. Paul's, 2004

Public and various as a shopping mall
At home, with as many knick-knacks for sale—
Probably Churchill's turning in his grave,
Which isn't here, just a slab of marble
Marking where his coffin stood. Mother soaks
Her aching spine at the hotel, too tired
For any more cathedrals, wanting to pack.
An ill-scheduled group of Germans, guided
To the American chapel—Churchill,
Half-Yank himself, turns again—hears its words
Of thanks translated, and I want to kneel:
How is a free life born? *Praise Him, All Ye Works
Of the Lord* arches overhead in Latin.
I ask for blessing in my mother tongue.

Antonioni's *Blow-Up*

Already dated when I'm in college,
David Hemming's bell-bottomed swagger
And talk of Nepal, the thick eyeliner
Raccooning his models: misogyny

Or a knight-errant's heart makes him walk out
Of one shoot, leave the models standing there
With eyes shut, arms artfully akimbo, bare
Bony torsos thrust sideways as they wait;

Already dated, the Mary Quant bangs
And white lips of two Twiggy wannabes
Who haunt his trail. The three fuck like bunnies
In one scene. It's all in fun. He hangs,

In his swank Knightsbridge flat, not fashion spreads
Or even portraits of the most gorgeous—
What happened to . . . was her name Veruschka?—
But poster-sized shots of London's rag-clad

Scrounging for fish and chips in curbside bins,
Sleeping in tube stations, sleeping in parks.
(Film 301. Late 70s. No talk
Of homelessness except after hurricanes,

Those fires and earthquakes covered on TV.)
Sleeping in parks. In a green leafy copse—
Even then my brain translated corpse—
A body lies waiting to be found. What's real

But the shots developed in his darkroom,
Characters and props taking hazy shape
As fixative scents the air, as blowups
Reveal a splayed leg flattening grass, an arm

Holding a gun, a woman's frightened face—*there*—
Then dissolve to grains? Or is the body,
And the gun, a trick of light? I'm twenty,
Taking notes as if the world might disappear.

from Manhattan Love Stories:
From The Millenium

1. Queensboro Bridge

Four fuming lanes of cars and taxis snake
Stalled from the intersection to farther
Than I can see; the driver's sweaty neck
Cranes out the side window, Black 47
Blasting immigrant rage from a cassette.
He settles back and shouts details of friends
Left behind in Cork, the tape now Costello;
"This is hell, this is hell," lyrics sweetly crooned,
As though he sang of heaven—"but you'll get used
To it . . . it'll never get better or worse"—
Or of this gridlocked traffic, cops short-fused
And bullhorning about an ambulance:
"Again, again," the siren screams; red lights
Flame the window. I'll never get used to it.

2. Itinerary

What's "mid-life" when every long distance call
And letter seem to shriek sad news or loss—
Abortion, cancer, AIDS, divorce; a car crash
That locks me sobbing in school bathroom stalls
Several times a week, though my colleagues
Grow less patient with each new month of tears;
Another friend's psychosis, one's eyes scarred
Near blindness—and some not even thirty?
Two years ago this spring, before L. bought
That rattletrap she died in, she took to pieces
A new poem I'd crowed about, its subject
A loved city: "Dull, distanced . . . what's the reason
You've left home? Girl, why don't you just say it?
You're choking there. You need to breathe again."

3. Houston Street Grille

Some gulp a tranquilizer when nervous;
My backpack's crammed with three vintage dresses
Costing more than airfare and my room combined,
Bought wildly on the morning's walk downtown.
At home, I'd sworn that our long-tended flame
Was dying low, another habit, shameful,
If less scorned here than post-lunch cigarettes.
Outside, punk lovers, young as my students
But tattooed, jostle my pack-laden arm
While we hug goodbye, their bare ones adorned
With portraits of Charles Manson and Hitler.
Why do these encounters possess such allure
When short, their farewells always chaste, like this?
He'll marry soon—I'll miss him, more or less.

4. Travel Permission

A day off from my prep school's hard to get—
All girls, taught mostly by females, most smart
Yet raised to be fulfilled with love, with friends,
To scant Milton and history for the heart.
The handbook lists our phone numbers; the girls
May call us anytime. And do. (We worry
When they don't.) A substitute's long-scheduled;
I type instructions for the VCR,
An intro for the Sylvia Plath tape,
Tidy my desk. Hours before the plane takes off
The phone rings, and a mom stutters my name:
Her child's been gone all week, but swastikas
Drawn on her locker were the cause, not flu.
Her best theme, on Anne Frank, misspelled *Dachau*.

DIANN BLAKELY *(June 1, 1957 - August 5, 2014)* was an American poet, essayist, editor, and critic. She taught at Belmont University, Harvard University, Vanderbilt University, the Watkins Arts Institute, and served as the first poet-in-residence at the Harpeth Hall School in Nashville, Tennessee. A Robert Frost Fellow at Bread Loaf, she was a Dakin Williams Fellow at the Sewanee Writers' Conference. She won two Pushcart Prizes and has been anthologized in numerous volumes, including Best American Poetry 2003. Her first collection, *Hurricane Walk*, was listed among the year's ten best by the *St. Louis Post-Dispatch*; her second book, *Farewell, My Lovelies*, was named a Choice of the Academy of American Poets' Book Society; and her third volume, *Cities of Flesh and the Dead*, won the Alice Fay Di Castagnola Award from the Poetry Society of America as well as the 7th Annual Publication Prize from Elixir Press. She was poetry editor at *Antioch Review* and *New World Writing*. Her poetry collection *Rain in Our Door: Duets with Robert Johnson* is forthcoming from White Pine Press, and *Each Fugitive Moment: Essays, Memoirs, and Elegies on Lynda Hull* is forthcoming from MadHat Press.

PAUL KLEE
LEGENDS OF THE SIGN

Interpretations in Art, No. 1

INTERPRETATIONS IN ART
A series of Columbia University Press

Mannerism and Anti-Mannerism in Italian Painting
Walter Friedlaender

PAUL KLEE
LEGENDS OF THE SIGN

RAINER CRONE

AND

JOSEPH LEO KOERNER

Columbia University Press
New York

Columbia University Press

New York   Oxford

Copyright © 1991 Columbia University Press
All rights reserved

Library of Congress Cataloging-in-Publication Data

Crone, Rainer, 1942–
    Paul Klee : legends of the sign / Rainer Crone and Joseph
Leo Koerner.
        p.   cm.—(Interpretations in art)
    Includes bibliographical references and index.
    ISBN (invalid) 0-231-07034-6 (alk. paper) : $25.00
    1. Klee, Paul, 1879–1940—Criticism and interpretation.
2. Signs and symbols in art. I. Koerner, Joseph Leo.
II. Title. III. Series.
ND588.K5C76   1991
759.9494—dc20   90-24618
                          ∞   CIP

Casebound editions of Columbia University Press books are
Smyth-sewn and printed on permanent and durable acid-free
paper

Printed in the United States of America

c 10 9 8 7 6 5 4 3 2 1

Contents

Preface

The work of translation made possible through the discovery of the Rosetta Stone in 1799 was not without its disappointments. In a letter to his brother August Wilhelm, the German romantic philosopher and poet Friedrich Schlegel registers an uneasiness about the new method of decoding the wisdom of the ancients:

> Please write me what you think of Champollion's system of hieroglyphs. It exerts a strong attraction on me, and I pass my time with it. The other side of matters—I mean the actual symbolic representation on Egyptian monuments—[Champollion] seems, of course, less to understand, possessing no real feeling for such things. These too can now be conquered, but only after all that which is pure script, along with those hieroglyphs that are mere letters, has first been wholly deciphered, and when this, taken by itself, is totally separated from the actual symbolic representations.[1]

Writing in 1825, just one year after François Champollion's epochal *Précis du Système hieroglyphique des anciens Egyp-*

tiens, Schlegel is justly enthusiastic about reading a body of texts that had been closed to Western culture since late antiquity. Yet he is also dissatisfied by what they are revealed by Champollion to *say.* Once deciphered, that is, hieroglyphics turns out to be a writing like any other known writing, its messages no deeper, its stories no more profound, than those of any other text. Against such demystification, Schlegel attempts to reoccult a sense of depth by positing another, more esoteric text behind the legible hieroglyphs, a text that he calls "symbolic." Within this domain, he recuperates what had finally, after millennia of false keys and pseudo-systems, been vanquished: the still-undecoded hieroglyph within whose essential untranslatability the "wisdom of the ancients" was, for the moderns, grounded.

Schlegel's faith in a symbolic representation which would be wholly distinct from script or letter rests upon the notion, foundational to romantic aesthetics generally, that a sign can so merge with its referent that it becomes untranslatable, being its own best possible formulation. Before such signs exegesis will be redundant or, as F. W. J. Schelling put it, "tautegorical." Within a tradition reaching back into the eighteenth century, this identity between signifier and signified, between what a sign says and what it means, is termed the symbol. Art is one of its privileged domains. For the early romantics, the Egyptian hieroglyphs represented a special case of the symbolic, for in their apparent combination of mimetic and non-mimetic elements, they were believed to be the remnants of a wholly natural langauge, in which word and meaning were absolutely one. That is, what was believed to be embodied by the hieroglyph were not only meanings of an unimaginably deeper, more mystical kind; the way it articulates those meanings, its mode of signification itself, was also believed to be more immediate, more symbolic, than any known language or sign system. Herein lay the source of its fascination: the hieroglyph told a legend which, by the very nature of its telling, could never be translated into our ordinary post-lapsarian languages, which separate word and object, being and meaning. With the Rosetta Stone and its utilization by Champollion, however, the hieroglyph lost this imagined privilege. The deciphered anicent texts might indeed now reveal unknown myths, religions, and histories, but they would do so in an ordinary manner, in a language like our own: not natural, but conventional, and never wholly symbolic.

In his late work entitled *Legend of the Nile*, Paul Klee seems to have absorbed the post-romantic hieroglyph's fall from grace (plate 23). Here is assembled a spectrum of signs from line and letter to cipher, pictogram, and landscape. On the one hand, these signs, all dwelling on the same patterned plane, appear fully conventional: the pinkish circle at the upper framing edge may mean "the sun above the sea," yet its matter is no different than, say, the x, v, or Greek pi below. It is a graphic mark, a pure line enclosing a circle, which denotes the sun. On the other hand, framed as if in a scene and placed upon the blue of sea and sky, all marks begin again to revive. The *Legend of the Nile* tells a modern story, in which the hieroglyph, having been revealed to be no more than convention, is reduced to almost pure form. However, in imitating the shape of Egyptian writing, Klee also invokes the Romantic project of the symbol, and with it the utopian belief in an art deeper than ciphers on a surface. To read such tablets, it will be necessary to decipher their script against a modern history of the sign.

The essays of this book analyze Klee's pictorial practices by placing them within the context of twentieth-century discussions of the nature and status of the sign. Far from being a whimsical *Kleinmeister* or a romantic modern, Paul Klee develops a thorough-going and radical critique of the grounds of visual representation. In his novel conjunctions of word and image (e.g., in the poem paintings and the late hieroglyphic works), his deconstructions of the dominant symbols of Western pictorial representation, and his emphasis on the material aspects of works of art, Klee extricates painting from its traditional, "naturalized" function: as representation of reality, expression of self, or construction of pure (i.e., non-mimetic and non-narrative) forms. In place of these stubborn fictions, Klee proposes the painting as sign, and thus as cultural praxis whose meanings and effects emerge diacritically, in the manner theorized for language by the Swiss linguist Ferdinand de Saussure.

The radicality of Klee's critique of the grounds of picture-making has been concealed by a history of art which tends to preserve a romantic notion of the image precisely overturned by Klee. The two essays that make up this book analyze the circumstances and consequences of Klee's break with tradition. Rainer Crone's essay establishes the historical and methodological basis for viewing Klee's art as a sign system in the sense proposed by Saussure. Saussurian linguistics here does not serve as a mere "methodology" for the interpretation of Klee; rather, Crone uncovers the hidden homologies between the thematization of language as sign in structuralist linguistics and Klee's pictorial project. Joseph Leo Koerner's essay, "Paul Klee and the Book," discovers the relation between Klee's pictures, read as signs, and wider cultural phenomena which are themselves analogous to the Saussurian reduction. The image of the book, which in literature (Joyce and Mallarmé) becomes linked to the question of the materiality of language, and in Klee's painting becomes the intrusion of writing into the domain of visual representation, serves as an ideal concrete example of the view of Klee proposed here. By letting the book be materialized as painting, and by submitting the painting to the textuality of the book, Klee blurs the boundaries between categories of cultural representation: image and word, nature and culture, thing and representation.

While different in style and focus, the two essays presented here are the product of an ongoing dialogue between their authors which dates back to a research seminar on Klee conducted by Crone in 1983 at the University of California at Berkeley. Convinced, with Schlegel, that hieroglyphs can never be fully translated, the authors each tell a legend among many legends of the signs of Paul Klee.

NOTES

1. Letter of April 27, 1825, *Friedrich Schlegels Briefe an seinen Bruder August Wilhelm,* edited by Oskar F. Walzel (Berlin: Speyer & Peters, 1890), p. 643.

Figures

FIGURE 1. Paul Klee, *Grid*.

Diagram from Klee, *Notebooks. Volume I: The Thinking Eye,* edited by Jürg Spiller, translated by Ralph Manheim (London: Lund Humphries, 1961), p. 217. © 1989, copyright by COSMOPRESS, Geneva.

FIGURE 2. Paul Klee, *The Carousel* (1889?).

Pencil drawing on paper, 11 × 14 cm. Collection Felix Klee, Bern. © 1989, copyright by COSMOPRESS, Geneva.

FIGURE 3. Paul Klee, *Fish*.

From Klee, *Notebooks* I:264. Upper fish (1 seen as *individual* and 2 seen *dividually*): pencil on paper; section: 9 × 8 cm; sheet: 28 × 22 cm. PN 5 (III) 188a *(Pedagogical Notebooks),* Paul Klee Foundation, Bern. Fish below (fish with scales): pencil on paper; section: 5.5 × 8.5 cm; sheet: 33 × 20.9 cm. PN 5 (III) 192a *(Pedagogical Notebooks),* Paul Klee Foundation, Bern. © 1989, copyright by COSMOPRESS, Geneva.

FIGURE 4. Paul Klee, *Form-giving examples with structures on dividual-rhythmical base and with individual accents.*

From Klee, *Notebooks. Volume II: The Nature of Nature*, edited by Jürg Spiller, translated by Heinz Norden (London: Lund Humphries, 1961), p. 211. Pencil and color crayon on paper. Several sections of one sheet newly arranged; sheet size: 27.3 × 21.5 cm. PN 17a Man 20, 59a *(Pedagogical Notebooks)*, Paul Klee Foundation, Bern. © 1989, copyright by COSMOPRESS, Geneva.

FIGURE 5. Paul Klee, *Hammamet with Its Mosque* (1914/199). Watercolor and pencil on paper. 20.6 × 19.4 cm. New York City, The Metropolitan Museum of Art, The Berggruen Klee Collection, 1984 (1984.315.4). © 1989, copyright by COSMOPRESS, Geneva.

FIGURE 6. Paul Klee, *Architecture Red-Green (yellow-purple gradations)* (1922/19).

Oil on canvas with red watercolor border around edges of canvas, laid down on cardboard mat. 34.4 × 40.3 cm; with border: 37.9 × 42.8 cm. New Haven, Yale University Art Gallery, Gift of Collection Société Anonyme (1941.533). © 1989, copyright by COSMOPRESS, Geneva.

FIGURE 7. Paul Klee, *Beginning Chill* (1937/136).

Oil on cardboard nailed on a frame, 73 × 53 cm. Private collection. © 1989, copyright by COSMOPRESS, Geneva.

FIGURE 8. Paul Klee, *Architecture in the Evening* (1937/138).

Oil on cotton, mounted, 60.5 × 45 cm. Private collection, photograph courtesy of Galerie Louise Leiris, Paris. © 1989, copyright by COSMOPRESS, Geneva.

FIGURE 9. Paul Klee, *Villa R* (1919/153).

Oil on cardboard, 26.5 × 22 cm. Basel, Oeffentliche Kunstsammlung, Basel Kunstmuseum. Inv. Nr. 1744. © 1989, copyright by COSMOPRESS, Geneva.

FIGURE 10. Paul Klee, *The Vocal Fabric of the Singer Rosa Silber* (1922/126).

Gouache and gesso on canvas, 51.5 × 42.5 (irregular). Collection, The Museum of Modern Art, New York. Gift of Mr. and Mrs. Stanley Resor. © 1989, copyright by COSMOPRESS, Geneva.

FIGURE 11. Paul Klee, *Once emerged from the gray of the night . . .* (1918/17).

Watercolor, pen drawing (in India ink) over pencil on paper cut into two parts with strip of silver paper between, mounted on cardboard, 22.6 × 15.8 cm. Paul Klee Foundation, Museum of Fine Arts, Bern. © 1989, copyright by COSMOPRESS, Geneva.

F I G U R E   1 2 .   Paul Klee, *Signs in Yellow* (1937).

Pastel on burlap, 96.3 × 50.6 cm. Basel, Collection Beyeler. © 1990, copyright by COSMOPRESS, Geneva.

F I G U R E   1 3 .   Paul Klee, *Let Him Kiss Me with the Kiss of His Mouth* (1921).

Watercolor over pen and India ink and pencil on paper, 16.1 × 23 cm. Lucerne, Angela Rosengart Collection (1921.142). © 1990, copyright by COSMOPRESS, Geneva.

F I G U R E   1 4 .   Paul Klee, *Document* (1933).

Oil, watercolor, and plaster on gauze and wood, 22.8 × 19.1 cm. Lucerne, Angela Rosengart Collection (1933.Z.3). © 1990, copyright by COSMOPRESS, Geneva.

F I G U R E   1 5 .   Paul Klee, *Plant Script Picture* (1932).

Watercolor on colored sheet, 25.2 × 52.3 cm. Bern Kunstmuseum, Paul Klee Foundation (1932.61). © 1989, copyright by COSMOPRESS, Geneva.

F I G U R E   1 6 .   Paul Klee, *Composition with Windows* (1919).

Oil over pen and India ink, varnished, on cardboard, 50.4 × 38.3 cm. Bern, Kunstmuseum, Paul Klee Foundation (1919.156). © 1989, copyright by COSMOPRESS, Geneva.

F I G U R E   1 7 .   Caspar David Friedrich, *Cemetery in the Snow* (1827).

Oil on canvas, 31 × 25.3 cm. Leipzig, Museum der bildenden Künst.

F I G U R E   1 8 .   Caspar David Friedrich, *View from the Studio of the Artist, Right Window* (1805/6).

Pencil and sepia, 31 × 24 cm. Vienna, Kunsthistorisches Museum.

F I G U R E   1 9 .   Paul Klee, *Open Book* (1930).

Gouache over white lacquer on canvas, 45.5 × 42.5 cm. New York, Guggenheim Museum. Photo: David Heald. © 1990, copyright by COSMOPRESS, Geneva.

Cosmic Fragments of Meaning:
On the Syllables of Paul Klee

RAINER CRONE

To Jonathan Miller,
as students become friends,
so friends become teachers

And, moreover, what about these conventions of language? Are they really the products of knowledge, of the sense of truth? Do the designations and the things coincide? Is language the adequate expression of all realities? —Friedrich Nietzsche (1884)[1]

One of the most significant of twentieth-century intellectual developments has been the growth of the modern science of linguistics, the study of "existing languages in their structures and in the laws revealed therein."[2] The enormous energies invested in probing the structure and function of language have produced insights of far-reaching influence. To speak of

The following essay would not have been realized without Jonathan Miller's fruitful dialogue. His thoughtful contributions to my 1978 seminar, "Paul Klee and the Theory of Sign" at Yale University, proved invaluable. The collaborator on both ideas and sentences, I am gratefully indebted to his modesty.

a linguistic revolution in our era is no exaggeration, for as Jacques Lacan indicates, "the reclassification of sciences and regrouping of them around it [linguistics] points up, as is the rule, a revolution in knowledge."[3] The effects of this "revolution in knowledge" are still filtering down into many areas of study.

The linguistic revolution has two aspects: "First there has been a massive development of synchronic linguistics whose particular object of knowledge is language's own laws of operation"; the counterpart of this first aspect is "the assumption that all social practices can be understood as meanings, as significations and as circuits of exchange between subjects and therefore can lean on linguistics as a model for the elaboration of their systematic reality."[4] The history of art figures prominently among those disciplines which would seem receptive to the second aspect of the linguistic revolution; certainly the social practice of artistic production can be understood within the compass of "meanings, significations, circuits of exchange between subjects." Yet art historical methods have adjusted slowly and unevenly to the type of understanding expressed in the linguistic model.

In *Art and Illusion* (1956) Ernst Gombrich, exploring the conventions which reign in artistic representation (an exploration intended to discredit naive notions of faithful renderings of "nature"), felt it necessary to state that "everything points to the conclusion that the phrase, 'language of art' is more than a loose metaphor."[5] Gombrich bases his examination of the "language of art" on the philosophy, rather than the science, of language, although he does take account of the latter. It now appears that any attempt to characterize art in terms of language has to confront the analytical methodology developed by linguistics and its corollary, semiotics.

Ferdinand de Saussure, whose *Cours de Linguistique Gén-*

érale (published posthumously in 1916) played a fundamental role in establishing modern linguistics, saw linguistics as forming a part of another more general science, one which had not yet been developed. This science, semiology (from the Greek *semeion*, or 'sign') would have as its concern "the life of signs within society."[6] (For the moment a sign may be defined as "everything which can be taken as significantly standing for something else.")[7] To Saussure it was obvious that language was "a system of signs that express ideas."[8] Language, while the most widely used, and the most exemplary, of sign-systems, is not the only one. Once constituted, semiology would subsume linguistics; the study of language would become a part of the study of sign systems:

> Semiology would show what constitutes signs, what laws govern them. . . . Linguistics is only a part of the general science of semiology; the laws discovered by semiology will be applicable to linguistics, and the latter will circumscribe a well-defined area within the mass of anthropological facts.[9]

Since Saussure, semiology or semiotics has developed along many disparate paths, most of them characterized by the same hypothetical tenor with which Saussure proposed the science's right to existence. Furthermore, Saussure's conception of the relation of linguistics to semiology has been called into question; it seems more apt to say that "linguistics is not a part of the general science of signs, even a privileged part, it is semiology which is a part of linguistics."[10] "All more or less hypothetically generalized" semiotic theories still rely heavily on a linguistic model, a dependency which gives rise to many obstacles in the consideration of social practices which are, properly speaking, non-linguistic.

This increasing conceptualization of social practices in terms of a linguistic model should be seen not as an academic fashion, but as a response to history itself. Only in the last

twenty-five years or so has semiotics developed rigorous for-
mulations, and for good reason.

> The deeper justification for the use of the linguistic model . . .
> lies in the concrete character of the social life of the so-called
> advanced countries today, which offer the spectacle of a world
> from which nature as such has been eliminated, a world
> saturated with messages and information, whose intricate
> commodity network may be seen as the very prototype of a
> system of signs. There is a profound consonance between
> linguistics as a method and that systematized and disembod-
> ied nightmare which is our culture today.[11]

The consonance between the linguistic method and twen-
tieth-century culture should not be limited to only the present
day. The elimination of "nature as such" from art took place
in the early years of this century.

The linguistic method seems eminently suited to consid-
erations of modernism in the visual arts for other reasons as
well. Because "the crucial and revolutionary aspect of mod-
ern linguistics is [its] insistence on the primacy of relations
and systems of relations,"[12] a further consonance opens up
between the linguistic method and the aesthetic credos of
many modern artists. Georges Braque's statement, "I do not
believe in things, I believe in relationships,"[13] and Paul Klee's
following statement exemplify this type of relational thinking
for the visual arts in the modern era: "A work should [not]
consist solely of elements. The elements should produce forms
but without losing their own identity. Preserving it. Usually
several of them will have to stand together to produce forms,
or objects or other secondary things."[14]

The consonance between the linguistic method and the
visual arts will be examined in the following sections. After
an introduction to the linguistic model developed by Saussure
and some of its implications, this discussion will lead into a

consideration of two aspects of Paul Klee's oeuvre: his architecture-paintings and his use of language in the symbolic space of the image.

II

From certain viewpoints it is not difficult to understand painting under the rubric of sign. If for the moment we adopt Umberto Eco's provisional definition of a sign—"a sign is everything which can be taken as significantly substituting for something else . . . everything which can be used in order to lie. If something cannot be used to tell a lie, . . . it cannot in fact be used to tell at all" [15]—it becomes clear that many works of art, particularly representational works, fall within this general definition. Throughout the greater part of its history, visual art has served to signify. The importance of visual imagery in the Middle Ages (stained glass, or *The Biblia Pauperum,* for instance) provides a striking example of this. Those members of society to whom the predominant sign-system—language—was inaccessible were granted access to cultural meanings through the signs of visual art.

With some adjustments, even a painting by Kandinsky or Malevich can be understood within the terms of the above definition. Kandinsky's improvisations around 1913 were to a large degree part of a highly personal, recondite sign-system; the forms he employed were linked (at least for him) to specifiable meanings. Malevich's works are, in general, signs of new conception of space and time, as developed in theoretical physics, and if this seems too broad a categorization of Malevich, certainly his forms evince the type of approach to relationships mentioned above, making them receptive to analysis by the linguistic model.

However, the complications attendant upon applying

semiotics to works of visual art are not so easily resolved. The language of painting is never given apart from individual works, and since the language of painting is not in the possession of the entire social body but of a limited number of individuals, it can undergo many more volatile mutations than language proper.

For theoretical purposes, the general characteristics of the language of painting can be designated by the term "tableau." This term best renders the sense of painting as a two-dimensional surface whose edges simultaneously bracket out the real and include the symbolic; a tablet which artists have inscribed more or less from the Renaissance to the present. The tableau circumscribes a distinct range of possible actions: singing at a blank canvas does not produce a painting, just as waving a paint brush in the air does not produce words. In recent years the tableau has seemed to many artists a limitation to be abandoned, a frame for the type of inscription to which they no longer feel impelled. One thinks of Duchamp's nausea at the "smell of oils and turpentine," and his decisive abandonment of painting for *chess* (among other activities), which Saussure used in his *Cours* as an analogue for the structure of language. Although it might have seemed that the bell tolled for the tableau in the early years of this century when the symbolic irrupted into the real (as with Duchamp), its death has been a slow one, and it is still valid to consider it as a locus of significations.

How semiotics, firmly rooted in a model derived from linguistics, may illuminate the signifying mechanisms of the tableau remains to be seen. Granting the tableau its status as a locus of signification (meaning), the question arises as to what characterizes the specificity of the tableau as opposed to other signifying systems and just how far semiotics takes us in defining that character.

As an introduction to the nature of the semiotic discipline, we may invoke Julia Kristeva's explanation of its main discovery:

> However great the diversity, the irregularity, the disparity even of current research in semiotics, it is possible to speak of a specifically semiotic *discovery*. What semiotics has discovered in studying "ideologies" (myths, rituals, moral codes, arts, etc.) as sign-systems is that the *law* governing, or, if one prefers, the *major constraint* affecting any social practice lies in the fact that it signifies; i.e., that it is articulate *like* language. Every social practice, as well as being the object of external (economic, political, etc.) determinants, is also determined by a set of signifying rules, by virtue of the fact that there is present an order of language.[16]

Kristeva introduces here the linguistic bias of semiotics. Unless qualified, her claim that the major constraint affecting any social practice is that it is articulated like a language can be deceptive. Kristeva's intent is not to declare unequivocally that these social practices are forms of language, only that they are *like* a language. As another critic of semiotics notes: "To be sure, when today we say that everything is ultimately historical, or economic, or sexual, or indeed *linguistic,* we mean thereby not so much that phenomena are made up, in their very bone and blood cells, by such raw material but rather that they are susceptible to analysis by those respective methods."[17] For semiotics to have discovered in studying social practices as sign systems that they are articulated like a language means that it has found its categories—based on the structure and function of language—to be applicable to a wide range of "anthropological facts." Painting should be counted among these facts, among the social practices, insofar as the works of individuals who acquire competence in the language-game of painting are circulated and exchanged, consumed by society.

Semiotics finds in language (as described by linguistics) a

model whose structural properties are generally analogous to nonlinguistic phenomena. To understand the oscillations of this analogy requires some knowledge of "language's own laws of operation." For the purpose of orientation in this field, we may examine the achievements of Saussure.

Saussure's primary gesture was "to introduce an order into the inchoate mass of speech acts that compose a language."[18] Saussure introduced this order by distinguishing between *langue* and *parole*. *Langue* is a synchrony, the total system of a language, "the ensemble of linguistic possibilities or potentialities at any given moment." It comprises the set of structural rules or limits for parole, "the individual and partial actualization of some of these potentialities."[19] *Langue* is the social institution; *parole,* the individual event.

The *langue/parole* relation can be phrased in other words as the systematic matrix of language and the individual acts which arise from, and are permitted by, that matrix. The subject who engages the system—plugs into it, gets socialized into it—finds expression therein, this expression manifesting itself as speech acts. *Langue* and *parole* are interdependent for definition: no acts of speech can be performed without the competence (both to generate and to understand expressions) supplied by the system and "the system only exists in the fact that the potential infinity of utterances is comprehensible."[20]

Semiotics postulates that "there exists a general category *langue/parole* which embraces all the systems of signs . . . (applicable) even . . . to communications whose substance is non-verbal."[21] The possibility presents itself that a *langue* could be identified for painting; the tableau circumscribes a general notion of the language system of painting. Whether it is possible in all rigor to define a *langue* for painting remains to be seen. What should be noted at this point is that Saussure's *langue/parole* relation has been broadened into the general notion that "behind every process one should be able to find a system."[22]

Saussure's distinction between institution and event shifted the focus of linguistics to the characteristics of the institution. "The linguistic system—what might nowadays be called the 'code'—pre-existed the individual act of speech, the 'message.' Study of the system therefore had logical priority."[23] The sign is the central fact of language as a system. For Saussure, the sign was a two-fold relation, uniting not "name" and "thing," but "sound-image" and "concept," or *signifier/ signified*. Saussure rejected a vertical approach to the sign, that is, in relation to its referent (the equivocal "thing"), in favor of a horizontal approach in which language comes to be seen as a structure—"an autonomous entity of internal dependencies."[24] Thus, the internal relation of signifier and signified composing the sign, and the relation of sign to sign become paramount. By excluding the referent from the consideration of the sign, Saussure established language as a system of signs that lies "parallel to reality itself."[25] With this, the "discussion of the bi-univocal correspondence between the word and the thing" gave way to the "study of relations proper to the signifier and the breadth of their function in the birth of the signified."[26]

Several things should be said about Saussure's conception of the linguistic sign. First of all, the relation between signifier and signified results from an arbitrary correlation established by convention. Here both notions, "arbitrary" and "convention," are equally important and far-reaching for their theoretical implication to painting, as we will see. No characteristic of the signifier/painting derives from the signified it articulates. The unmotivated connection between signifier and signified is known as the arbitrary nature of the linguistic sign— a much disputed fact, as Roman, Jakobson, one of the first critics, pointed out.[27] One might be led by this to think that language is just a nomenclature applied to preexisting concepts, but as Jonathan Culler points out, Saussure warned against this facile conception of language:

> A language does not simply assign arbitrary names to a set of independently existing concepts. It sets up an arbitrary relation between signifiers of its own choosing on the one hand, and signifieds of its own choosing on the other. Not only does each language produce a different set of signifiers, articulating and dividing the continuum of sound in a distinctive way, but each language produces a different set of signifieds; it has a distinctive and thus "arbitrary" way of organizing the world into concepts or categories.[28]

This brings us to a second aspect of Saussure's conception of the linguistic sign: "Both signifier and signified are purely rational or differential entities."[29] Saussure felt that it was impossible to designate an absolute unit in linguistics; language is best conceived of as two correlated systems, a system of expressions and a system of contents. As such there are no units with fixed essences, only values and relationships resulting from the interaction of the two correlated systems:

> In a state of system there are no absolute terms, only relations of mutual dependence. Saussure expressed it, "language is not a substance but a form." And, if the intelligible form *par excellence* is opposition, then again with Saussure, "in a language there are only differences." This means that we need not consider the meanings attached to isolated terms as labels in a heteroclite nomenclature. What we are to consider are only the relative, negative, oppositive value of signs with respect to each other.[30]

The form of language is characterized by differential oppositions of distinctive units (phonemes). The correlation of signifier and signified does not fully encompass the identity of the sign; signs are produced just as much by value, the relation of one signifier to other signifiers, one signified to other signifieds.

Saussure illustrated the concept of value in linguistics by the analogy of a sheet of paper: if one cuts the paper into strips, each one of the pieces—as well as having two sides (recto/verso, signifier/signified)—has a value in relation to its neighbors. Thus, "the signifier cuts out, articulates a certain space which becomes through this articulation a signified, that is, meaning."[31] The relationship of signifier and signified and the articulation and division of the "sound image" and "concept" continua should be seen as strictly intertwined.

Finally it becomes necessary to point to a "profound structural dissymmetry in the couple signifier/signified. The first of these seems able to exist as a kind of free floating autonomous organization, while the other is never visible to the naked eye."[32] The fact is that whenever one goes in search of the signified, the signifier appears in its place; in order to specify what Saussure calls a concept, one must replace it with a sound-image, signifier replacing signified in a process of "unlimited semiosis." For instance, specifying the signifieds of a tableau means replacing its signifiers with a text of verbal signifiers. Likewise, if we specify what the word "tree" means by drawing an image of a tree, we have again merely replaced signifier with signifier.

Jacques Lacan has called Saussure's formula of *signifier/signified* "a pure function of the signifier."[33] Semiotics should be differentiated from semantics on this ground: the former refers to the plane of expression (signifier), the latter to the plane of content (signified). The dissymmetry between signifier and signified effectively focuses attention on the signifier. For, as Lacan says, in order to keep in view the question of language's very nature, one must "get rid of the illusion that the signifier answers to the function of representing the signified or better, that the signifier has to answer for its existence in the name of any signification whatsoever."[34] From this approach to the signifier arose Lacan's notion of "an incessant sliding of the signified under the signifier,"[35] and Julia Kristeva's notion of *signifiance:* "The flux of meanings across a textual surface, its free play of signifiers which is to be distinguished from communication- and denotation-bound 'signification.' "[36] These two notions can be understood by reference to the general term "polysemia," the overdetermination of the sign, the pool of potential signifieds upon which the signifier floats.

Because of the continual flight of the signified, the object of semiotics is the structure of the signifier, whose characteristics are as follows:

> Now the structure of the signifier is, as it is commonly said of language itself, that it be articulated. This means that no matter where one starts from in order to describe the zones of reciprocal infringement and the areas of expanding inclusiveness of its units, these units are submitted to the double condition of reducing to ultimate distinctive features and of combining according to the laws of a closed order.[37]

The ultimate distinctive features of the linguistic signifier are phonemes; the combination according to the rules of a closed order Lacan calls the signifying chain, "rings of a necklace that is a ring of another necklace made of rings,"[38] an image which eloquently renders the sense of the process of signification as an expansion of interlocking articulations, a simultaneous gearing up and gearing down.

Because painting relies on a different physical/psycho-physiological circuit than language, the structure of the signifier in the tableau differs from the linguistic signifier. The painter's "utterance" depends on the hand which arranges the "stuff of art," a process considerably different from producing "flawed words and stubborn sounds" (Wallace Stevens, "The Poems of Our Climate"). Furthermore, the signifying chain in language unfolds in a line (even if in certain cases, e.g., poetry, language's multi-dimensionality gets stressed), whereas in reading a tableau, we find the "writing" there to be transcursive, multidirectional, simultaneous. The visual aspect of writing certainly deserves examination, which we will do in analyzing Klee's poem-painting *Once Emerged From the Grey of Night;* it seems subject to a closed order of rules in essentially the same material conditions that determine graphic art (the pencil which traces the letter is also capable of image-making),[39] the latter subject to an "open order" of rules.

The fundamentals and some of the implications of Saussure's linguistics have been sketched here to indicate the nature of the linguistic model. In mapping that model onto the language-game of painting certain transformations must occur:

> If painting lets itself be analyzed in terms of system[s], system is not necessarily to be understood as system of *signs,* and . . . that if the problematic of the sign can be revealed as pertinent in the matter, at its level and within its proper limits, this is perhaps to the extent that the notion of *sign* lets itself be disjoined from that of *system* (and reciprocally). Unless it is perhaps for us to work to impose another notion of sign, another notion of system, than those which all the Western tradition will have regularly associated with the possibility of cutting a whole, an articulated structure, into discrete elements, into units identifiable as such.[40]

The traditional concepts of both system and sign oscillate when viewed in light of the tableau. Semiotics' reliance on the linguistic model gives rise to several problems. Linguistics biases semiotics to consideration of the system, the social institution. The separation of *langue* from *parole* runs the risk of ignoring not only the ability of those who engage the system to renew it and to alter it, but also those instances where indeed there is no system to be decisively extrapolated from the infinity of speech acts. To introduce the *langue/ parole* distinction in painting "will always be a matter of sketching a surface of cleavage between the performance which a work represents (the 'masterwork') and the network, if not the system of competences which are put into play by the deciphering of the work, its interpretation—and all that even though one posits that 'art' is never given apart from individual works, that its significance does not refer to any recognized code or convention and that the signifying relations of 'artistic language' are to be discovered at the interior of a given composition."[41] The system appears after the fact in painting; we read it into the infinity of works which continually change the conditions of that reading. Painting does not draw upon a closed order of distinctive features to produce its signifiers, if it weren't for convention as such and conventional schemes of reception. So if there is a system (competence) underlying the individual work (performance), it is one which continually renews itself.

Because the tableau problematizes the system, the notion of sign must be reassessed as well. Setting up language—"the most powerful semiotic device that man has invented"[42]—as a master pattern can easily obscure the specific character of nonlinguistic signs. Whereas "all signs consist of a signifier and signified, a form and an associated meaning or meanings," not all signs may be said to possess the same arbitrary nature of the linguistic sign, nor do they necessarily arise from "cutting a whole, an articulated structure into discrete elements."[43]

It therefore becomes essential to distinguish between different types of signs, as did Charles S. Peirce, the American philosopher who had already developed a complex semiotic theory by the late nineteenth century,[44] by establishing the classification that "a sign is either an icon, an index or a symbol."[45] Peirce's "symbol," a somewhat misleading term, corresponds to Saussure's arbitrary sign; Peirce speaks of a "contract" by which the symbol functions as a sign. In an icon "the relation between signifier and signified is not arbitrary but is one of resemblance or likeness."[46] Saussure believed that even if semiology were to take account of "natural signs," such as icons, "wholly arbitrary signs are those which come closest to the semiological ideal."[47] It has proved very difficult to identify very many sign systems outside of language which are based on the principle of arbitrariness;[48] those which have been found—"micro-codes" such as semaphore, Morse code, traffic signs—articulate "a very sparse semantic range."[49] To undermine this "verbo-centric dogmatism," all considerations of visual art have to come to terms with the notion of iconism, with signs not wholly arbitrary.

III

> Roland Barthes once said that the work of art *"est une forme que l'historie passe son temps a remplir."* I agree with this statement, but I would prefer to re-translate it into the categories of the present semiotic approach; the work of art is a text that is adapted by its concrete addresses so as to fulfill many different communicative purposes in diverse historical or psychological circumstances, without ever completely disregarding the underlying rule that has constituted it.
>
> *—Umberto Eco*[50]

The paths travelled in the preceding section can now converge on their ultimate destination: specific examples of the painter's practice. Several of Paul Klee's architecture-paintings as well as examples involving his use of language inside the pictorial space have been chosen for this purpose.

In Klee's architecture-paintings we face, without question, iconic texts. It is possible to speak of these works in terms of recognizable contents, without ever having to enter into debates about their faithfulness to nature; they hover between abstraction and representation, orchestrating both the "seen" and the "known." More importantly, Klee's architecture-paintings evidence the development of a systematic *articulation* of the tableau. These works depend for the most part upon an implied, if not actually present, division of the pictorial surface into a grid. The fact that this method of formal articulation circumscribes a particular set of contents—architectural contents—suggests the presence of a coding correlation. Although the product of an identifiable underlying rule, it should be clear that these works evidence only one specific approach to the generation of iconic texts, a particularly notable approach for our purposes because it is *systematic*.

Architectural themes preoccupied Klee throughout most of his career. We can pick up the thread of his attention to architecture as early as 1903.[51] Reflecting on the influence exerted on him by Renaissance architecture in Italy, Klee noted in his diary the importance of architecture as a school of form:

> When I learned to understand the monuments of architecture in Italy, I won an immediate illumination. Although these are utilitarian structures, the art of building has remained more consistently pure than other arts. Its spatial organism has been the most salutary school for me. . . . Because all the interrelations between their individual design elements are obviously calculable, works of architecture provide faster training for the stupid novice than pictures or "nature." And once one has grasped the idea of measurability in connection with design, the study of nature will progress with greater ease and accuracy.[52]

Klee's insight into the connection of measurability with design and his sense of architecture as a *spatial organism* provided the impetus for his architectural abstractions. But many years passed before he began to effect the fusion of "the architectonic and the poetic"[53] in his work.

During the years 1903 to 1914 Klee assiduously applied himself to mastery of the basic formal means of line, tone, and color, integrating each element methodically. He gathered inspiration for his formal investigations from contact with the post-Impressionists—Cezanne ("the teacher *par excellence*")[54], Matisse, Van Gogh, and later (circa 1911–1914), the Cubists—with Delaunay making the greatest impression on Klee. In 1914, Klee travelled to Tunisia on a lark and his experience there represents a critical point in his career. Before turning to the "synthesis of urban architecture and pictorial architecture,"[55] which Klee commenced in Tunisia, two important concepts from his teaching at the Bauhaus deserve attention.

In his *Contribution to a Theory of Pictorial Form*,[56] under the heading of "Constructive Approaches to Composition," Klee introduced a distinction between the "dividual" (by which he means a divisible structure composed of repeated elements) and the "individual" (a nondivisible organism). Klee had come to understand this distinction many years earlier, as the following diary entry from 1905 attests:

> Individuality is not an elementary sort of thing, but an organism. Elementary things of different sorts coexist in it, inseparably. If one tried to separate them, the components would die. My self, for instance, is a dramatic ensemble. Here a prophetic ancestor makes his appearance. Here a brutal hero shouts. Here an alcoholic *bon vivant* argues with a learned professor. Here a lyric muse, chronically love-struck, raises her eyes to heaven. Here papa steps forward, uttering pedantic protests.

Here the indulgent uncle intercedes. Here the aunt babbles gossip. Here the maid giggles lasciviously. And I look upon it all with amazement, the sharpened pen in my left hand. A pregnant mother wants to join the fun. "Pshtt!" I cry, "You don't belong here. You are divisible." And she fades out.[57]

This quote is noteworthy not only because it introduces the concepts of dividuality and individuality—the individual an organism composed of "elementary things of different sorts" —but also because it illustrates the schizophrenic self-consciousness of central importance to Klee's work: the dramatic ensemble of the self fills the stage of his imagination.

As Klee formulated it in his *Pictorial Theory,* the *dividual* is characterized by being "purely repetitive and therefore structural."[58] The simplest dividual structures result from the repetition of "unaccented elements" like the regular pulse of a musical beat, or a single course of bricks. The dividual reduces to the equation: $I+I+I+I$, etc.[59] Klee's example of a more complex dividual structure is the intersection of parallel vertical and horizontal lines to form a grid or diagram (the unaccented elements repeated in two directions) (figure 1). In such a structure any number of parts may be attached or removed without changing its rhythmic character which is based on repetition: "elementary things" repeated indefinitely and without accent build dividual structures and so the dividual can be typified as indeterminate number. In this respect, note how *Carousel,* a childhood drawing, depends on dividual structures—the fringe on the rim of the carousel's top, the dashes and dots of its center structure (figure 2).

Dividual structures can consist solely of line or line and tone value: the unaccented grid is a purely linear example; if we turn it into a checkerboard, we merely create a composite dividual element (black and white + black and white $= 1 + 2 + 1 + 2 = I + I$, etc.) In the checkerboard the unaccented repetition of a higher dividual element still results in a dividual structure. Klee further characterizes dividual structures as nonorganic; they may compose organisms but are not organic in themselves. As Klee said to his students:

> In the structural sphere we have gone through an exercise from which nothing has emerged that is false, true enough, but neither has it given rise to anything particularly lively. Rather what has come out has been on the rigid ornamental side.[60]

An *individual,* on the other hand, has definite measure, determinate extension (cf. indeterminate number, dividual); nothing can be added to or subtracted from it without changing it radically, "without disturbing or even destroying the function of the whole,"[61] putting it to "death." For this reason the individual is organic as opposed to the non- or suborganic dividual. Individuals have a character beyond rhythm, which can be described in terms of proportion, quality, and intensity.

Klee illustrates individuality with the example of a fish (figure 3). Head, body, tail, and fins compose the fish's proportions; add or subtract one of its parts and the individual dies.

Klee goes on to show how the dividual and the individual are synthesized. The individual itself may be composed of dividual structures. The fish "seen as an individual breaks down into head, body, tail and fins. Seen dividually it breaks down into scales and the structure of the fins."[62] Properly speaking, the individual structure is born through the "intimate fusion of individual and structure"[63] (individual proportion and dividual structure); the identity of the fish depends on its proportions, but those proportions are fused with the repetition of elementary units. This fusion reaches "the limit of the perceptible," the letter of the image: "Perceptibility does not go beyond this limit, but remains within the perceptible whole, entering into its parts, its dividual rhythms."[64]

Pursuing the dividual/individual synthesis further, Klee asks:

> But is the fish always an individual? No, not when it occurs in large numbers, not when "it is teeming with fish," as the saying goes. When it's teeming with fish, we have not one fish but many, we have a fish-pond or an aquarium.[65]

Thus dividual structures compose individuals and these individuals can in turn become the elementary units of a higher perceptible whole.

At this point it is worth recalling that from his earliest youth Klee attached major importance to the principle of analogy. He regarded it as one of the most effective aids for understanding the interconnection of ever more complex facts. An analogy exists between mathematics and the structural system of a plant. There is an analogy between nature and the creative act, and yet another between pictorial and urban architecture—and many other examples.

Klee invokes another highly pertinent analogy for the relationship between the individual and the accompanying dividuum, one which suggests without doubt he must have had knowledge of recent achievements in linguistics. In 1916, Saussure's *Cours* was published in Lausanne and reviewed in every major Swiss newspaper as a centennial achievement of a noted Swiss scholar in structural linguistics. One of these reviews appeared in the Sunday papers in Klee's hometown of Bern.[66] Paul Klee, fluent in French, might very well have read these celebrated lectures of Saussure's, available to the public in the format of Saussure's students' notes.[67]

> The longer and more indefinite the series, the easier it is to add or subtract a few without making any essential change in

the exhibit. In the same sense I can line up series of concepts (e.g., sound, syllable, word, sentence, etc.).

The concepts lower (or dividual) and higher (or individual) are not absolute but mutally dependent; when I broaden the conceptual field, I create a higher perceptible whole.[68]

Klee links the structure of language to the structure of pictorial form by finding in each a hierarchy of levels in which lower, dividual levels are continually integrated into higher, individual levels. A principle of relationship reigns here loosely comparable to Lacan's image of the signifying chain—up to the higher perceptible whole, the morpheme (and further, the text), down to the building blocks, the *figurae*. We begin to see here the truth of Kristeva's analogy—the articulation *like* a language—even if the characteristics of language's articulation can't be mapped point for point onto nonlinguistic phenomena. In Klee's opinion, the two levels of formal articulation were practically inseparable, although for the purpose of analysis they could be separated. Even though, as Klee says,

the line between singular articulation and mass articulation must lie somewhere, it is less important to localize this precisely than to regard the two elements as being in contrast, e.g., the singular as moving forward, the masslike as moving backward.

The disparity between the two then leaps to the eye. The mass element I should like to call structural character. The articulated aspect of mass should be envisaged as the massive repetition values that are of a similar order of smallness.[69]

The structural character of language may also be understood as the massive repetition of values that are of a single magnitude. The passage from mass to singular articulation is of central importance for the creative act. The artist must always keep his eye on "the higher proportions of individual structure"; they are "form-determining," whereas dividual structures are "form-realizing." The ultimate form a work takes results from the mutual cooperation between the governing proportions and "the pliable material aspect" of the indefinitely extending structures.[70] We can most clearly see this in the approach to composition, which Klee termed "partially constructive figuration."

An illustration of this approach to composition (diagram) —one essential type of the dividual/individual synthesis— occurs in Klee's notes: "Form-giving examples with structures on dividual-rhythmical base and with individual accents" (figure 4). The individual accents conform strictly to the dividual matrix in these examples; the structural norm establishes the constraints within which "free choice" may take place. The interplay of systematic constraint and free choice parallels that of *langue* and *parole,* as defined by Saussure. Free choice, individual accent in Klee's examples, generates protoimages, the limit of the perceptible. Partially constructive figuration "avails itself of a schematic basis (norm) from which it chooses what it deems suitable for free figuration. . . . The partially constructive manner happens to be productive in a form-creative sense but only by calling on the help of the destructive principle. The creative ruin."[71]

Klee's architecture-paintings epitomize the dividual/individual synthesis as it appears in the method of partially constructive figuration; in them a schematic basis serves as a departure point for free figuration.

In the Tunisian watercolors, Klee was already employing a partially constructive method. In *Hammamet with Mosque* (1914) (figure 5), an implied if not actually present grid, a dividual basis, lays the ground for the creation of the image. A combination and opposition of colors and lines serves to create the impression of a landscape with architecture, bathed in light. Topographical clarity is ensured, earth and sky being apparent at a glance. However, the schematic division of the surface into grid-like rectangles, triangles, and squares seems an unusual aspect to include in a landscape. The vertical strip composed of orange, yellow, blue, and white, running down the right-hand side, can be regarded as an indicator of this basic grid: it divides the surface into horizontals and verticals. The top edge of the watercolor, where Klee inserted a narrow red-rust, red-yellow strip, detached from the lower edge and turned around by 180 degrees, functions similarly. In fact, Klee defines the upper third of the painting by the two towers placed against the light blue–white section of the background, which continue the form and color used in the basic grid pattern. But he diverges from the dominant vertical/horizontal pattern of the surface with three undulating diagonal lines, initially drawn in pencil. These diagonals add movement to a composition, what Klee might have referred to as a construction, in a painting whose structure might otherwise produce a more static effect. These diagonals, the flowing sand dunes of the desert, serve as space-creating coulisses. Klee creates a mosque from the schematic basis by extending a pale violet band into the "sky," the sparsely painted upper portion of the field.

The basic structure of this watercolor reveals a more or less schematic division of the picture plane into horizontals and verticals, producing a number of rectangles and squares, and with slight modifications, triangles. It is only when the artist applies his brush to provide graphic details that the picture acquires its definition, and clarifies what is intended to be up and down. These details transform geometrical shapes into architectural forms, into towers and minarets, before our eyes. Klee is using only the sparsest of means, and turns colored patches into gardens and fields, using figures in an abbreviated, suggestive form, reducing them to pure signs. On the other hand, plants are depicted in a figurative manner. In conjunction with the signs placed in the bottom half of the picture, the round dots next to the mosque allow us, the spectators, to associate these sections with something more objective; whether this calls to mind gardens, tufts of grass, groups of people, or window openings in the minarets is immaterial. It is more important to recognize that this represents the emergence of a new way of perceiving and planning paintings: the pattern or network of coordinates comprising verticals and horizontals, forming the basis of the entire pictorial structure. Using only a limited number of additional graphic elements, it is possible to impose the face on a landscape, a momentary impression on this structure—a structure which itself determines the whole, as Klee stated in his diary of July 1917.

"The creative ruin" may now be better understood. To bypass the rigidity of dividual structures, and to engage creative freedom of choice, the schematic basis must be destroyed. The individual takes precedence over the dividual; it prevails at the expense (or absence) of the dividual. Integrally dependent on this process is a progression from the static to the dynamic, a progression from a purely dividual, static structure to a structure beyond rhythm, irregular, dynamic. We may imagine a battle, immanent in the work and the process of its creation, between the conservative dividual faction which fights under the banner of static order, the norm, and the radical individual faction whose declared ideology is dynamic movement, deviation from the norm. As we watch the battle, we can see creation creating itself.

All the elements of free figuration in *Mosque*—the color ("quality," therefore individual), the diagonal deviations from the grid, the linear activity of the flora, the architectural details—serve to individualize the dividual basis. The process of individualization produces the image as such, the visual text. The letter of the image results from the elements, which individualize the grid; so, *taken as a whole* the deviations from the norm *signify*. The difference between the norm, the system, and the individual, the figuration, generates meaning.

To a large degree, the abstract quality of *Mosque* can be ascribed to the underlying construct which asserts itself apart from any representational function. The patches of color in the image fluctuate between depiction, indicating features of the landscape from which Klee painted, and an autonomous existence as pure pictorial elements, released from the demands of representation to become parts of a construction.[72] The tension between depiction and construction evidenced by *Mosque* emphasizes the very nature of an iconic sign: culturally coded yet not wholly arbitrary.[73]

The uneasy coexistence of opposing functions in the pictorial elements of *Mosque* can be ascribed to the grid structure itself. As Rosalind Krauss has pointed out,

> In the spatial sense, the grid states the autonomy of the realm of art. Flattened, geometricized, ordered, it is antinatural, antimimetic, antireal. It is what art looks like when it turns its back on nature. In the flatness that results from its coordinates, the grid is the means of crowding out the dimensions of the real and replacing them with the lateral spread of a single surface. In the overall regularity of its organization, it is the result not of imitation, but of aesthetic decree. Insofar as its order is that of pure relationship, the grid is a way of abrogating the claims of natural objects to have an order particular to themselves.[74]

The striking quality of *Mosque* results from the fact that Klee painted with nature *en face:* the anti-mimetic means of the grid serve mimetic ends. In a sense *Mosque* embodies the contradictions of modernist art at the early stages of its development: the antinomies of construction and depiction locked in a single focus, an order of pure relationships generating the dimensions of the real.

As might be expected, when Klee became a form-master at the Bauhaus, the constructive element came to the fore in his work. Klee painted *Architecture Red/Green (yellow-purple graduation)* in 1922 close to the time he presented the dividual/individual relation in his course at the Bauhaus (figure 6). Whereas *Hammamet with Mosque* was painted from the motif, in *Architecture Red/Green* Klee turns his back on nature, or in other words, the grid predominates. Because it is unlikely that Klee began with a regular division of the surface, the grid does not exist as such. Only one or two of the verticals and horizontals go from edge to edge uninterruptedly; the imaginary regular grid has been made dynamic by shiftings and subdivisions. However, the imaginary regular grid "provides a solid basis on which to consider the action in the picture as a whole and in its parts. Starting from the norm, freely chosen steps are taken leading to irregularity."[75] The result of these deviations from the norm in *Architecture Red/Green* is a complex interplay (interrelation) of different sized planes. Smaller rhythms build up into individual parts, which in turn join larger rhythms. The movement produced by the irregular projection of the grid is further enhanced by irregular color rhythms; greens and reds heightened and muted respectively by yellow and purple.

By reducing composition to a systematic basis in which every variation from the system has expressive value, Klee created a visual text in which a simple act performed by a single element—a diagonal, for instance—embodies a wealth of associations. Two qualities of *Architecture Red/Green* and its structure incorporate architectual associations. First, in the irregular projection of the grid the verticals are closer together than the horizontals, giving rise to an overall impression of verticality. The upright rectangles become parts of facades, piers, sides of buildings. Likewise, the curved and straight diagonals—further departures from the norm—produce arches, cornices, and even roofs. This production of meaning should be referred to Eco's discussion of the iconic sign/text: "A graphic convention allows one to transform . . . the schematic conceptual or perceptual convention which has motivated the sign." [76] The "graphic" or pictorial convention in this case is Klee's systematic approach to composition which is designed to encode the elements of a conventional conception/perception of vernacular architecture.

The space in *Architecture Red/Green* is more ambiguous than in *Hammamet with Mosque*. Larger elements seem to project, smaller ones recede; the half-arches and cornices suggest respectively front and side views. The overall movement subverts the cues which would allow the space to be read rationally. Because the image tends to flatten out ("flattened, geometricized, ordered" [Krauss]) as well as push and pull, every attempt to construct a rational space fails. Whereas *Mosque* depends on a more or less traditional topology (upper part of the field corresponding to sky and so forth), *Architecture Red/Green* dispenses with the dimensions of the real, operating on the basis of a multidimensional simultaneity. Like Picasso's *Still Life with Violin and Fruit Bowl* (1913), for example, Klee's architecture scrambles recognition codes in a flight from appearances. Klee's basic credo, "art does not reproduce the visible, but makes visible," locates him without the artistic context which established the autonomy of the iconic text. The interrelationships of different values, not the particular resemblance of the visual text to any real-world referent, create the significance of *Architecture Red/Green*.

Klee's admiration for Picasso's most recent production of collages, such as his *Still Life with Violin and Fruit Bowl*, goes back at least to 1914 when he created the collage/painting

Homage to Picasso using an oval format similar to Picasso's first collage of 1912, *Still-Life with Chair Caning.* The writings of the more penetrating art critics of the time may help us to understand the change in the mode of pictorial practice in the early twentieth century, and thus shed light on the direction that Klee's artistic development increasingly took from 1914 on.

In his Berlin lecture on Delaunay, for example, Apollinaire noted that

> this art was concerned with painting new combinations of formal elements, derived not from visual reality, but from concepts. This tendency leads to a poetic kind of painting placed outside the scope of observation: . . . to produce a picture: one which, even were an effort made to understand it, would be entirely divorced from the object, i.e., the objective reality which one was seeking to present.[77]

Maurice Raynal, without doubt one of the period's most perceptive critics, wrote about the exhibition *La Section d'Or* in October 1912 as "the idea of conceptually conceived painting, which has taken over from paintings of visible things."[78] He emphasizes "the principle of painting things the way one thinks of them, and not the way they are perceived by the shortsighted." He rejects descriptive or anecdotal, moralizing or sentimental, pedagogic or decorative painting. His major essay "Conception et Vision," written in August 1912, states that, in endeavoring to attain the truth, it is not simply a matter of "apparently imitating nature." Instead we must rely on those things we comprehend. Rejecting Italian Futurism and its studies of motion in painting, Raynal regarded "painting based on external perception" as insufficient. In the search for truth, he considered "conceptual notions" a means of a more adequate presentation of reality. It is only by introducing "a conceptual notion . . . that we can imagine objects that we are unable to see. In the moment of entertaining the conceptual notion of a book I do not perceive it within a certain dimension, but with all dimensions together. If a painter succeeds in presenting an object in all its various dimensions, he is accomplishing the work of a higher order than one painted only in its visible dimensions."[79]

Klee's views on the way abstraction functions support the above conception of the autonomy of the visual text:

> Within the will to abstraction something appears that has nothing to do with objective reality. Free association supplies a key to the fantasy and formal significance of a picture. Yet, this world of illusion is credible. It is situated in the realm of the human.
>
> Memory, digested experience, yields pictorial associations. What is new here is the way the real and the abstract coincide or appear together.[80]

Klee's understanding of this abstraction recalls Eco's critique of the supposed similarity of the perceptual results produced by a photograph and an actual object. Eco claimed that on the basis of previous learning (memory, digested experience), two different perceptual results were viewed as "one and the same" perceptual result.[81] The painter's practice does not rely on the same strict transformational rules as the photomechanical process and therefore the thread linking the two perceptual results is susceptible to attenuations and splits. Even if in *Architecture Red/Green* the perceptual result does not too closely resemble everyday coded perception of actual architecture, the real and the abstract conicide on the level of content (pictorial associations).

Interpretations, such as that offered by Christian Geelhaar, which overemphasize the constructed character of Klee's architecture-paintings, risk mistaking the nature of Klee's abstraction:

> It would be too easy to interpret the colored squares simply as
> bonded masonry, triangles as tower roofs, crescents as domes,
> but such interpretations remain superficial. Like the Master
> Builder, the painter is striving to form a construction "capable
> of carrying the load."[82]

While it is important to emphasize the construction in these
works, Klee's construction process should be seen within the
parameters of a general process whereby a coding correlation
is proposed. The ease with which interpretations such as
cornice, arch, etc, suggest themselves is telling. It points out
that these constructions maintain a certain semantic link with
actual architecture and the fact that Klee had achieved a
mechanism communicated as much. Ignoring the coinci-
dence of the abstract and the real on the planes of expression
and content can only result in a superficial formal interpreta-
tion.

The breadth of meaning which Klee could incorporate into
the architectural format appears full force in a late work,
Beginning Chill (1937) (figure 7). This work is very much part
of the romantic symbolism of death which filled Klee's last
works. Based on the same vertical/horizontal division of the
surface as *Hammamet with Mosque* and *Architecture Red/
Green, Beginning Chill* employs this structuring principle in a
different way. Six major verticals and horizontals divide the
field into nine areas. In five of these areas (the four corners
and the center), blues, grays, and greens predominate; in the
other four, yellow, oranges, and browns. Within each of these
areas various dividual rhythms build up, always in the service
of creating architectural meaning. In the lower right corner of
the center area, a rhomboidal lattice creates a window shut-
ter; the middle area at the top is given over to the sweeping
activity of pointed roofs; in the area to the immediate right of
the center area, bright orange and yellow lozenges (the high-

est values of any in the picture) suggest decorative tile work or distant roofs. All these various elements enter into relationships with surrounding elements and forms, cohere and dissolve, open up and flatten out space. Meanings flow across the textual surface. In the lower left area a figure extends a craggy limb towards a window in what appears to be an interior space. The figure stands cut off from the outside, squeezed by the weight of the surrounding architectural activity. The colors wind down from a few sparks of fire, to ice, stone, and moss. In light of what has been said here about the individual, it is interesting that the figure is cut in half by the boundary between inside and outside. The pressure of the towering exterior crowds the individual into a constricted interior.

Here we move beyond the letter of the image. The figure, although apparently female, suggests Klee himself. This actor in the dramatic ensemble of his self has a darker resonance than the "lyric muse, chronically lovestruck" of many years earlier who "raises her eyes to heaven." In 1933, the Nazis locked Klee out of his Düsseldorf studio, forcing him to flee to his native Switzerland. By 1937, Klee's health was failing and even though his last years were among his most prolific, he would soon no longer expend his energies on such tightly ordered constructions as *Beginning Chill*.

Another architectural work, which comes after *Beginning Chill* in Klee's meticulously ordered work catalog, *Architecture in the Evening* (1937) (figure 8), depends on a much broader articulation of the surface. The grid confidently asserts itself, having completely colonized the surface in the names of construction.[83] The suggestion of architecture is more generalized, the significant linear deviations fewer; evening falls upon the architecture in *tempo adagio*. The resonances with Klee's stage in life are insistent.

IV

The support the title gives this work (and all discussed so far) brings up a point often stressed about Klee: the interrelation of title and work, the linguistic and iconic, in the production of meaning. One of the achievements of the Renaissance was the banishment of language from the symbolic space of the image. In the twentieth century language no longer merely flanks the boundaries of the tableau, or stands as an absent verbal text behind the iconic text; it brazenly enters symbolic space of the tableau, often tryannizing that space. The cubists invaded the tableau with random fragments of language in order to anchor their abstractions at the threshold of the intelligible. Klee's use of language, deriving from the cubist tradition, is multifaceted and deserves examination in the context of this discussion.

In *Villa R* (1919) (figure 9), the flat green *R*, a solid striding presence flanking the villa, which quietly echoes its forms, creates both a visual and phonetic identity for the scene. An *R* sound reverberates through the fantasy theater/landscape. Even though the letter seems integrally attached to the villa, it steps uneasily into the landscape, flattening the river-road which disappears into the distance, and casting no shadow as do the plants which surround it. The *R* is of a different order, a different dimension, than the rest of the scene: a dimension both linguistic and iconic. Here the letter of the image includes an image of a letter.[84]

The *Vocal Fabric of the Singer Rosa Silber* (1922) (figure 10) involves a somewhat more complex interrelationship between the linguistic and the iconic. Weaving up and down over the surface of the gently articulated (phantom grid) cloth are the vowels of the Roman alphabet, *a, e, i, o, u,* and above them two consonants, *R* and *S*. The vowels are song, airy voice, the primary tools of the singer's art. *R* and *S* function

FIGURE 1. Paul Klee, *Grid.*
Diagram from Klee, *Notebooks. Volume I: The Thinking Eye,* edited by Jürg
Spiller, translated by Ralph Manheim (London: Lund Humphries, 1961), p.
217. © 1989, copyright by COSMOPRESS, Geneva.

FIGURE 2. Paul Klee, *The Carousel* (1889?).
Pencil drawing on paper, 11 × 14 cm. Collection Felix Klee, Bern. © 1989, copyright by COSMOPRESS, Geneva.

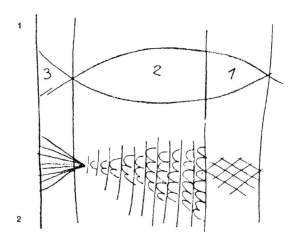

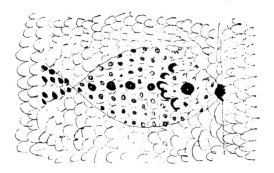

FIGURE 3. Paul Klee, *Fish.*
From Klee, *Notebooks* I:264. Upper fish (1 seen as an individual and 2 seen dividually): pencil on paper; section: 9 × 8 cm; sheet: 28 × 22 cm. PN 5 (III) 188a *(Pedagogical Notebooks),* Paul Klee Foundation, Bern. Fish below (fish with scales): pencil on paper; section: 5.5 × 8.5 cm; sheet: 33 × 20.9 cm. PN 5 (III) 192a *(Pedagogical Notebooks),* Paul Klee Foundation, Bern. © 1989, copyright by COSMOPRESS, Geneva.

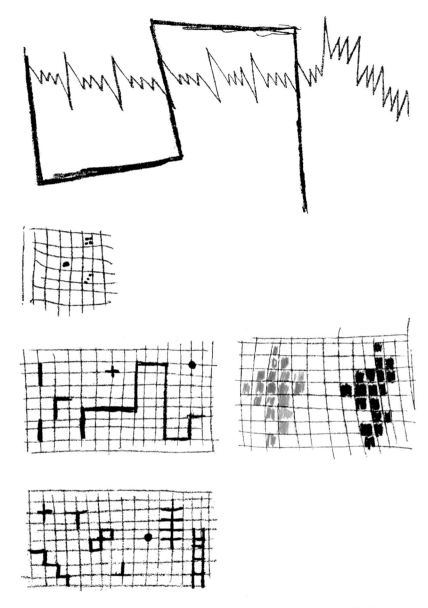

FIGURE 4. Paul Klee, *Form-giving examples with structures on dividual-rhythmical base and with individual accents.*
From Klee, *Notebooks. Volume II: The Nature of Nature,* edited by Jürg Spiller, translated by Heinz Norden (London: Lund Humphries, 1961), p. 211. Pencil and color crayon on paper. Several sections of one sheet newly arranged; sheet size: 27.3 × 21.5 cm. PN 17a Man 20, 59a *(Pedagogical Notebooks),* Paul Klee Foundation, Bern. © 1989, copyright by COSMO-PRESS, Geneva.

FIGURE 5. Paul Klee, *Hammamet with Its Mosque* (1914/199). Watercolor and pencil on paper. 20.6 × 19.4 cm. New York City, The Metropolitan Museum of Art, The Berggruen Klee Collection, 1984 (1984.315.4). © 1989, copyright by COSMOPRESS, Geneva.

FIGURE 7. Paul Klee, *Beginning Chill* (1937/136).
Oil on cardboard nailed on a frame, 73×53 cm. Current ownership un-
known. © 1989, copyright by COSMOPRESS, Geneva.

FIGURE 8. Paul Klee, *Architecture in the Evening* (1937/138). Oil on cotton, mounted, 60.5 × 45 cm. Current ownership unknown, photograph courtesy of Galerie Louise Leiris, Paris. © 1989, copyright by COSMOPRESS, Geneva.

FIGURE 9. Paul Klee, *Villa R* (1919/153).
Oil on cardboard, 26.5 × 22 cm. Basel, Oeffentliche Kunstsammlung, Basel
Kunstmuseum. Inv. Nr. 1744. © 1989, copyright by COSMOPRESS, Geneva.

in much the same way as the *R* in *Villa R:* to name, to identify the vocal fabric as that of Rosa Silber. Furthermore, the canvas support peeking through the gesso ground, the *fabric* of the image, speaks in unison with the title—"vocal-fabric"—to encode a figure of speech into the material of visual art. The vocal fabric sings not only through the inscription of letters on its surface, but through its linear, tonal, and textural modulations as well.

Seven letters float upon a vertical format. They are set, painted, upon a fabric. The loosely woven canvas and varying application of paint gives the work a highly tactile appearance. The adherence of the canvas to the backing, too, is done in such a way as to emphasize its material and constructional quality. The coloring is subtle, yet variegated. The canvas itself has been painted in vertical overlapping and fusing rectangles, some of which are dotted, cross-hatched, or lined, reversing dark on light and light on dark. The mottled background provides the ground for the floating letters. The colors of the seven letters blend with the tones of the background, but are a more intense hue of what we find in the ground.

Presented frontally, right side up as one would read them, the letters are concentrated in the center of the composition Privileged among the seven, the initials *R* and *S* are in capitals and read left to right in the upper portion of the picture. The *S* is larger than the *R* and seems to slip from the imaginary straight line on which the *R* is placed. Above it hangs a large black dot, possibly the indication of a period. Both initials are of the same rust color and are drawn in the same ordered form. This specific manner is straight-edged and straight-lined with thickening of the letter in principal areas. The lower case letters conform to similar construction.

The line of the initials is separated by a space which is initiated, like an indentation, by a black rectangular block which continues outside of the picture plane. Falling just below this piece are the *e*, in the same black, and the *i*, in an opposite white outlined black. The *o* and the *a* lie directly below the *RS* and are in the same rust tone while the *u* floating alone at right is in green. Taking the picture apart, with the title in mind, the letters fall into two groups: capitalized consonants and lower case vowels. Next to *RS*, the identification of *Rosa Silber*, in alphabetical order, are *a-e-i-o-u*, the five vowels. According to our rehearsed recitation of them, they are jumbled, but easily recognized. Unlike the initials, the vowels are of uniform size, approximately half the size of the initials, and do not read in sequence from left to right. What is the essential element in word construction and, consequently, speech and singing? The vowel. The vowel is the structuring force of word formation and the substance of singing. The act of singing, in fact, can be performed by vowel alone, but it cannot exist purely on consonants. The consonant itself, when made into an auditory image (our phonetic pronounciation), never gets away from the vowel (*B = be; L = el*, etc). In this way, the five vowels are what identify Rosa Silber as a singer and allow her to sing.

These same vowels signify singing apart from Rosa Silber, but Klee has taken the idea further by including *RS* in the same mode of representation. The painting is, after all, about one particular person, who according to Grohmann greatly impressed Klee.[85] The capitalization of *RS*, then, seem appropriate. It is in this way, that the painting operates in the self-reflexive mode, as the *RS* signifies Rosa Silber, Rosa Silber can also signify singing, which can signify *a-e-i-o-u* . . . and so forth. Klee presents two frozen signifying elements from a constant flow. Like a painting held up to a mirror, both elements *(RS* and *a-e-i-o-u)* signify concepts, but each element holds the concept within it and reflects it upon the other.

Though Klee's presentation of Rosa Silber seems somewhat

peculiar, it is quite conventional in itself. He defines *RS* first and foremost and defines it below. Nothing obstructs our view of it, not even its own presentation, for we are cued by the capitals and are given a straightforward, readable view.

In Klee's title the phrase "vocal fabric" calls to mind more than one concept. A fabric is something constructed, so that fabric stands here as a metaphor for a visual construction: a representation for something auditory. At the same time, vowels are the structure of, or the "fabric" for, singing. "Fabric" operates in a double sense *RS,* as identification, together with *a-e-i-o-u,* stands for the verbal representation of what is, as an entity, the fabric, the cloth, the gesso that signifies what Rosa Silber, the singer, is. On the other hand, *a-e-i-o-u* is the substance and thus the fabric of what we would hear from Rosa Silber. What we have here are the vowels as the fabric for language or sound and their physical sign as the fabric for visual representation. As the tactile quality of the painting becomes apparent to us, we sense a parallel projection from the singing of Rosa Silber. By depicting his signs as such and addressing the title to them, Klee represents in the fullest sense the voice of Rosa Silber, the substance of a singing Rosa Silber.

This graphic literalization of voice qualities should be seen in reference to what Eco calls rendering the matter of the sign-vehicle "semiotically interesting."[86] The matter of the tableau has been significantly valorized down to the lower limits of its articulation. In *Rosa Silber* the linguistic level coexists with the visual: letter, title, and visual image are set into motion to produce a unique synesthetic effect. The interdependence of these elements, their contextual solidarity—if the letters were removed, the surface handled differently, it would alter the identity of the work—makes clear the incestuous affair between the linguistic and the iconic.

The Vocal Fabric of the Singer Rosa Silber incorporates two of the functions of the linguistic in relation to the iconic: the anchoring function and the relay function.

> The linguistic message's anchoring function has a "repressive" value. Language is there to fix the always polysemic image's signifieds. It answers the question: what is it? . . . The relay function implies that the image and language are in a complementary relationship: language says what the image does not express.[87]

In *Rosa Silber* we can see how the polysemic image is anchored by its title. Without the title, the image would be wildly polysemic; too many meanings would converge upon the question "what is it?" With the title, its meaning is specified, "repressed." The relay function can be seen in *Rosa Silber* insofar as "the linguistic code and the optic code cohabit a space governed by the optic code alone."[88] The presence of language in the symbolic space of the image expresses the voice, something that is almost impossible without recourse to language. But, as we have noted, the image also means "voice," so perhaps it is better to say in reference to the relay function that language expresses what the image cannot express *in language*.

In *Einst dem Grau der Nacht enttaucht* . . . (1918) (figure 11)[89] the relay function predominates; images of letters inscribed in a dividual grid of colored squares contribute to the creation of the letter of the image. The complex play of meanings which the language system expresses can only be echoed schematically by the pictorial structure—the silver band in the middle of the field from which the colors and letters leap. The title is the poem which is the picture, a complex relay. The image/text reads as follows:

EINST DEM GRAU
DER NACHT

ENTTAUCHT
DANN SCHWER
UND TEUER
UND STARK
VOM FEUER
    ABENDS
VOLL VON GOTT
UND GEBEUGT

NUN ATHERLINGS
    VOM BLAU
UMSCHAUERT
ENTSCHWEBT
UBER FIRNEN
    ZU
KLUGEN GESTIRNEN

The poem can be translated thus:

Once emerged/from the gray of night
Then heavy/and dear
and strong/with fire
At evening/full of God/and bent.
Now towards heaven/showered about/by blue
Vanished/over the glaciers
To/wise stars.

This image of *Einst dem Grau der Nacht enttaucht* . . . throws into contrast Klee's systematic articulation of the tableau and the articulation of language; the two are held in a fugitive single focus, within the armature of the grid. As such, *Einst dem Grau* condenses in a single figure the two major themes we have explored: the articulation of the linguistic and the iconic. The tension between the two in this work suggests the representation of a struggle: the impossible desire of the iconic for the linguistic and vice versa.

Klee's dividual articulation in *Einst dem Grau* adapts itself well to the structure of letters (the hand which draws the letter makes the image). The tableau's potential infinity of articulations are reduced to an order of pure relationship closely allied to that of language. A letter in this image can suddenly become a colored square divided horizontally *(E)* vertically *(T)* or diagonally *(N)*. The colors jam the reading of the letters, as if consuming language in the process of trying to become like it. The tableau no longer opens onto nature, only onto itself. Lying parallel to reality, ever more arbitrary and autonomous, it tries to seduce that truly autonomous entity, language, by wrapping itself in the coordinates of a grid. But the attempt leaves everything in flux: words and images do not cohere; they cancel one another out in a way that we may never truly fathom.

Perhaps only in those cases where an order of pure relationships, a massive repetition of *values* of similar magnitude has been imposed on the tableau, is it proper to speak of the coincidence of linguistic and iconic articulation. But in *Einst dem Grau,* where such a case occurs, the dissociation of the iconic is clearly apparent. So we have to wonder about strictly transposing the structure of natural language onto the tableau, whether such an operation does not obscure the order of language which functions in the tableau.

For Klee, reaching the level of the perceptible, making a visual text, was always a matter of some form of articulation, even if undiscernible and asystematic. The statement from his "Creative Credo" (1918) that "abstract formal elements are put together like numbers or letters to make concrete beings or abstract things; in the end a formal cosmos is achieved."[90] exemplifies this. Cosmos is order, opposed to chaos, but it seems to be achieved here by reading itself to a closed order of distinctive features.

To define a universally valid *langue* for painting escapes our capacities. Even if we can examine isolated systems and the speech acts, the visual texts, they generate, we are unable to reduce painting to a combination of distinctive features. At best we can say, searching for syllables in the distances of sleep, the painter corrals them within the constraints of the tableau, giving us the many letters of the image, which we have always already gone beyond.

NOTES

1. Friedrich Nietzsche, *Werke,* edited by Karl Schechta (Munich: C. Hanser, 1954–1956; 3 vols.), 3:311.

2. Jacques Lacan, "The Insistence of the Letter in the Unconscious," in Richard de George and Fernande de George, eds., *The Structuralists* (Garden City, N.Y.: Doubleday, 1972), p. 290.

3. Ibid., pp. 290–91.

4. John Coward and Rosalind Ellis, *Language and Materialism* (London: Routledge & Kegan Paul, 1977), p. 1.

5. E. Gombrich, *Art and Illusion* (Princeton, N.J.: Princeton University Press, 1969), p. 87.

6. Ferdinand de Saussure, *Course in General Linguistics,* translated by Wade Baskin (New York: McGraw-Hill, 1966), p. 16.

7. Umberto Eco, *A Theory of Semiotics* (Bloomington: Indiana University Press, 1976), p. 7.

8. Saussure, *Course in General Linguistics,* p. 16.

9. Ibid.

10. Roland Barthes, *Elements of Semiology,* translated by Annette Lavers and Colin Smith (New York: Hill and Wang, 1978), p. 11.

11. Fredric Jameson, *The Prison-House of Language* (Princeton, N.J.: Princeton University Press, 1972), pp. viii–ix.

12. Jonathan Culler, *Ferdinand de Saussure* (New York: Penguin Books, 1976), p. 126.

13. Braque, as quoted in ibid., p. 128.

14. Paul Klee, "Creative Credo," in *Notebooks. Volume I: The Thinking Eye*, edited by Jürg Spiller, translated by Ralph Manheim (London: Lund Humphries, 1961), pp. 77–78.

15. Eco, *A Theory of Semiotics*, p. 7.

16. Julia Kristeva, "The System and the Speaking Subject," in *The Tell-Tale Sign: A Survey of Semiotics*, edited by Thomas A. Sebeok (Lisse: Peter de Ridder Press, 1975), p. 47.

17. Jameson, *The Prison-House of Language*, p. viii.

18. Coward and Ellis, *Language and Materialism*, p. 12.

19. Jameson, *The Prison-House of Language*, p. 22.

20. Coward and Ellis, *Language and Materialism*, p. 12.

21. Barthes, *Elements of Semiology*, p. 25.

22. Louis Hjelmslev, as quoted in Paul Ricoeur, "Structure, Word, Event," in *The Philosophy of Paul Ricoeur* (Boston: Beacon Press, 1978), p. 110.

23. Peter Wollen, *Signs and Meaning in the Cinema* (Bloomington: Indiana University Press, 1969), p. 117.

24. Hjelmslev, as quoted in Ricoeur, "Structure, Word, Event," p. 110.

25. Jameson, *The Prison-House of Language*, p. 33.

26. Lacan, "The Insistence of the Letter," pp. 291–92.

27. For a critique of the "arbitrariness" of the signifier, see Roman Jakobson, *Six Lectures on Sound and Meaning*, translated by John Mepham (Cambridge, Mass.: MIT Press, 1978), p. 51; Adam Schaff, "De la specifité du signe verbal," in *Language et Connaissance. Suivi de six essais sur la philosophie du langage*, translated by Claire Brendel (Paris: Editions Anthropos, 1969), pp. 319–36; Adam Schaff, *Introduction to Semantics*, translated by Olgierd Wojtasiewicz (Oxford; Pergamon Press, 1962), pp. 76–84.

28. Culler, *Ferdinand de Saussure*, p. 15.

29. Ibid.

30. Ricoeur, "Structure, Word, Event," p. 110.

31. Coward and Ellis, *Language and Materialism*, p. 13.

32. Jameson, *The Prison-House of Language*, p. 145.

33. Lacan, "The Insistence of the Letter," p. 295.

34. Ibid., p. 292.

35. Ibid., p. 297.

36. Kristeva, as defined by Hubert Damisch, "Eight Theses for (or Against?) a Semiology of Painting," in *Enclitic* 3(1):2, 1979.

37. Lacan, "The Insistence of the Letter," pp. 295–96.

38. Ibid., p. 296.

39. As clearly Klee himself was aware. See his letter to Lily Klee of March 22, 1916: "Such poems, mostly drawn linear with a pen, which I want to publish one day in book form, you should not give to Goltz. I want to keep these works for myself for the moment." In Felix Klee, ed., *Briefe an die Familie* (Cologne: DuMont Schauberg, 1979), 2:794.

40. Damisch, "A Semiology of Painting," p. 3.

41. Ibid., p. 2.

42. Eco, *A Theory of Semiotics,* p. 174.

43. See Wollen, *Signs and Meaning in the Cinema,* p. 122.

44. See Klaus Oehler, "An Outline of Peirce's Semiotics," in Martin Krampen, Klaus Oehler, Roland Posner, and Thure von Uexküll, eds., *Classics of Semiotics* (New York: Plenum Press, 1987), pp. 1–21.

45. Peirce, as quoted in Wollen, *Signs and Meaning in the Cinema,* p. 122.

46. Ibid.

47. Saussure, as quoted in Culler, *Ferdinand de Saussure,* p. 99; see also Saussure, *Course in General Linguistics,* p. 68 (for original text, see Ferdinand de Saussure, *Cours de linguistique generale,* edited by Tullio de Mauro [Paris: Payot, 1986], p. 100); Mauro's remarks on "convention" and "arbitrariness," ibid., p. 442.

48. See n. 27 for a critique of the "arbitrariness" of the signifier.

49. Wollen, *Signs and Meaning in the Cinema,* p. 118.

50. Eco, *A Theory of Semiotics,* p. 310.

51. Not to mention *Carousel* in which Klee's later style—repetitive structures, balanced constructions, fantasy—lies latent.

52. Paul Klee, *Diaries* (Berkeley: University of California Press, 1964), p. 146.

53. Ibid., p. 125.

54. Ibid., p. 237.

55. Ibid., p. 287.

56. Klee, *Notebooks,* vols. I and II.

57. Klee, *Diaries,* pp. 176–77.

58. Paul Klee, *Pedagogical Sketchbook,* translated by Sibyl Moholy-Nagy (London: Faber and Faber, 1953), p. 23.

59. Klee, *Notebooks,* I:217–22.

60. Paul Klee, *Notebooks. Volume II: The Nature of Nature,* edited by Jürg Spiller, translated by Heinz Norden (London: Lund Humphries, 1961), p. 293.

61. Ibid., II: 229.

62. Ibid., II: 264.

63. Ibid., II: 238.

64. Ibid., II: 264.

65. Ibid., II: 264–65.

66. Eco, *A Theory of Semiotics,* p. 206; see also the chapter on the reception of the *Cours* in 1916, as presented by Thomas M. Scheerer, *Ferdinand de Saussure* (Darmstadt: Wissenschaftliche Buchgesellschaft, 1980), pp. 30–36.

67. Klee would not have needed to read Saussure, though it is most likely that he did, since from 1917 onwards we find an increasing number of paintings and drawings which deal with the intricate relationships between letters, words, and numbers and pictorial structure (see his poem-paintings). Through a number of his close friends in Bern, scholars in literary history, Klee could have had access also to Georg von der Gabelentz' *Die Sprachwissenschaft. Ihre Aufgaben, Methoden und bisherigen Ergebnisse,* 2d ed. (Leipzig: Tauchnitz, 1901), the classic study on linguistic theory, one which is widely regarded as being extremely influential for Saussure's results, since it points out for example the difference between *langue* and *parole;* see, e.g., R. Hiersche, *Ferdinand de Saussures langue-parole-Konzeption und sein Verhältnis zu Dürkheim und von der Gabelentz* (Innsbruck, 1972).

68. Klee, *Notebooks,* I: 265–66.

69. Ibid., II: 37.

70. Ibid., II: 283.

71. Ibid., II: 32.

72. Note the tendency of the vertical band on the right to detach itself from the rest of the composition, as described above.

73. Eco, *A Theory of Semiotics,* p. 192.

74. Rosalind Krauss, "Grids," *October* 9: 51, 1979.

75. Klee, *Notebooks*, I: 235.

76. Eco, *A Theory of Semiotics*, p. 194.

77. Edward Fry, *Der Kubismus* (Köln: DuMont Schauberg, 1966), p. 120.

78. Ibid., p. 106.

79. Maurice Raynal, "Conception and Vision," in ibid., p. 95.

80. Klee, *Notebooks*, I: 262, 291.

81. Eco, *A Theory of Semiotics*, p. 193.

82. C. Geelhaar, *Paul Klee and the Bauhaus* (Greenwich, Conn.: New York Graphic Society, 1973), p. 48.

83. Although by no means for the first time in Klee's oeuvre. See *Architecture (yellow-violet stepped cubes)* (1922), *Resonance of the Southern Flora* (1927). This latter work indicates how the regular grid can be individualized solely through color movement and how the grid format can encode other than architectural contents.

84. For a fuller analysis of this painting, see Joseph Koerner, "Paul Klee and the Image of the Book," pp. 45–84 below.

85. Will Grohmann, *Paul Klee* (New York: Harry Abrams, 1955), p. 48.

86. Eco, *A Theory of Semiotics*, p. 266.

87. Michel Rio, "Images & Words," *New Literary History* 7(3): 509, Spring 1976.

88. Ibid.

89. Essential for an understanding of the following thoughts on *Einst dem Grau der Nacht enttaucht . . .* is the careful and elaborate description of this watercolor, a product of my graduate seminar on Paul Klee in 1983 (University of California, Berkeley). See Koerner, pp. 56–65 below.

90. Klee, "Creative Credo," in *Notebooks* I: 79.

Paul Klee and the Image of the Book

JOSEPH LEO KOERNER

I

What sort of sign has Paul Klee constructed in his 1937 painting entitled *Zeichen in Gelb (Signs in Yellow)* (figure 12)? On one hand, Klee has fashioned a pattern of yellow and orange planes that covers the whole surface of the composition up to the gray framing border. Although these rectangular forms vary in size and are not arranged in any strict order, the horizontal and vertical lines that their borders describe, and that often carry through the painting, structure the picture's space. On the other hand, here and there, outlining and sometimes entering into the space of the colored shapes are black linear figures. While these hieroglyphic forms assume a variety of shapes, from the simple dot or line to the complex figure, say, at the center of the picture's upper edge, they seem all to speak the same language. In 1922 Klee wrote of his own art: "For the most part we deal with combined forms. In order to understand combined forms one must dismember them."[1] *Zeichen in Gelb* combines black figures and colored planes in its composition, and it is difficult to discern which of these two distinct pictorial elements rules. For instance, the black lines seem in certain places to accommodate themselves to the structure formed by the planes, while elsewhere they appear to subvert the rectilinear structure of the painting: an edge of a colored plane is only curved where there is a curved line delimiting it. And while at first sight it seems that many planes stand free from any contact with a black figure, closer observation reveals that hardly a single plane is not somewhere bounded or at least touched by a black line. (The two squares that are not quite bordered by a line actually stretch out at their appropriate edge to establish some contact.) One of our pleasures as viewers resides in observing and testing out this conceit: watching how the yellow patches are indeed caught in the apparently loose and random web of black lines allows us to experience a secret reciprocity between apparently disparate systems. Like the relationship between the dividual and individual elements of a painting as formulated by Klee himself, the two pictorial components of *Zeichen in Gelb* appear to strike a "compromise"[2] in structuring and being structured by one another. Klee goes further than this, though, in sharpening the dialectic between the hieroglyphic lines and their colored ground.

Klee entitled his composition *Zeichen in Gelb,* rendering the strict polarity between figure and ground unstable. The painting might be read as an arrangement of black "signs" *in* a yellow field, or, conversely, the true signs might be *written in* yellow paint and are only separated or interrupted by the accompanying black shapes. *Zeichen in Gelb,* or *Yellow Signs* as it is usually called in English, asserts that the sign exists exactly where the "written" forms (the black hieroglyphs) *are not,* or better, that the sign emerges only diacritically, through the necessary combination of figure and ground in which each term is dependent on the other. Significance becomes located in the interruption between what we thought were written signs, between lines, letters, words, or books.[3]

Klee's overturning of figures and ground, letter and page, as it were, finds a useful parallel in the Jewish mystical tradition and its meditation on the origin of writing. According to the talmudic *aggadah*, prior to creation the whole Torah was written in black figures on white fire. Later interpretations from the thirteenth century onward came to regard the white fire as the true text of the Torah. It follows then that the authentic written Law has become completely invisible to human vision and is concealed now in the white parchment of the Torah scroll, the black handwritten letters being nothing more than a commentary on this vanished text.[4] Like Klee's *Yellow Signs,* this legend brings into question the ground against which signs are readable. Writing becomes a play of presence and absence: words and letters are only visible and therefore meaningful in their *difference* from the surface upon which they are written. In the Jewish story of the white fire, as in Klee's painting, we see that where we thought we saw a figure on a ground, we find that ground is itself a figure or a sign.[5]

It is easy to locate such meditations within contemporary theories of the sign. Since Ferdinand de Saussure, language and writing are regarded as being diacritical, as being meaningful insofar as they are expressed within a relation, i.e., between signifier and signified, *langue* and *parole,* diachrony and synchrony, etc. It is in the play of differences that reading and interpretation becomes possible. The story of the white and black fire refers specifically to the practice of interpretation. What we read, the black letters of the Torah, constitutes only a *commentary* on a hidden text. It is interesting that the overturning of figure and ground in Klee is also instantiated in a form of commentary or writing outside the image. For it is the title, a text absent from, yet informing the image, that forces us to read the painting as a composition of yellow signs.

It may seem strange that we should speak of Klee's composition in terms that are more appropriate for a discussion of writing or the book than for an interpretation of a painted image. Yet Klee's juxtaposition of signs against a neutral ground (or rather, of significant ground against sign-like shapes) is perhaps closer to the structure of writing than it is either to "nature" or to the tradition of illusionistic painting in the West. In nature we do not privilege one object as being more real or more significant than another, except insofar as nature itself is regarded as a book. And in Western painting since the Renaissance, figure and ground, or rather "objects" placed in the foreground and "objects" located further back in illusionistic space, tend not to constitute two separate spheres of signification but inhabit merely unique positions in the *res extensa*. Cartesian "continuous" space that formed the basis or ground for the pictorial tradition since the Renaissance gives way in Klee's art to a painting composed through the deliberate combination of two discontinuous systems—black linear figures and colored planes. While such a move might be relatively new within the history of painting, Klee's composition and the issues it raises have resonance within the very long tradition of discourse about the nature of writing and the book. It is within this discourse that we shall situate our discussion of Paul Klee's "signs."

II

The question of the book as a metaphor or cultural idea has assumed an important place within contemporary philosophy and critical theory. The book has not only come to be regarded as *the* exemplary vehicle for the transmission of

FIGURE 6. Paul Klee, *Architecture Red-Green (yellow-purple gradations)* (1922/19).
Oil on canvas with red watercolor border around edges of canvas, laid down on cardboard mat. 34.4 × 40.3 cm; with border: 37.9 × 42.8 cm. New Haven, Yale University Art Gallery, Gift of Collection Société Anonyme (1941.533). © 1989, copyright by COSMOPRESS, Geneva.

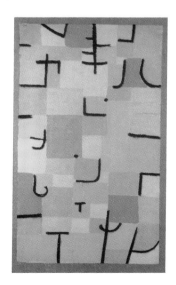

FIGURE 12. Paul Klee, *Signs in Yellow* (1937).
Pastel on burlap, 96.3 × 50.6 cm. Basel, Collection Beyeler. © 1990, copyright by COSMOPRESS, Geneva.

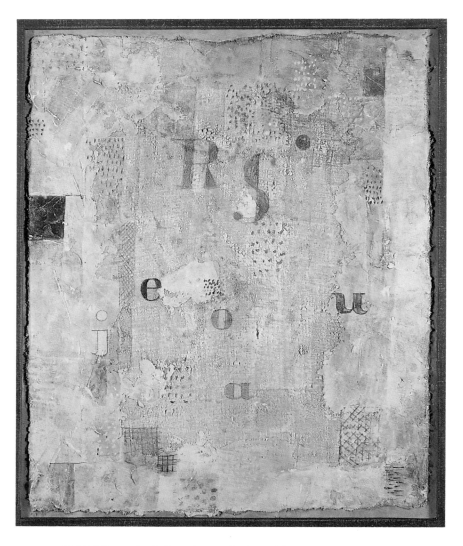

FIGURE 10. Paul Klee, *The Vocal Fabric of the Singer Rosa Silber* (1922/ 126).
Gouache and gesso on canvas, 51.5 × 42.5 cm. (irregular). Collection, The Museum of Modern Art, New York. Gift of Mr. and Mrs. Stanley Resor. © 1989, copyright by COSMOPRESS, Geneva.

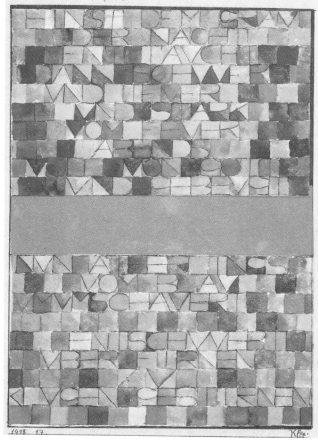

FIGURE 11. Paul Klee, *Once emerged from the gray of the night* . . . (1918/17).
Watercolor, pen drawing (in India ink) over pencil on paper cut into two parts with strip of silver paper between, mounted on cardboard. Paul Klee Foundation, Museum of Fine Arts, Bern. © 1989, copyright by COSMO-PRESS, Geneva.

FIGURE 16. Paul Klee, *Composition with Windows* (1919). Oil over pen and India ink, varnished, on cardboard, 50.4 × 38.3 cm. Bern, Kunstmuseum, Paul Klee Foundation (1919.156). © 1989, copyright by COSMOPRESS, Geneva.

culture. From the early writings of Maurice Blanchot to the work of Jacques Derrida, the dismantling of the form of the book, enacted within radical literary forms in which such dismantling is itself expressed, has also become a primary locus of the critique of culture as a whole.[6] In the "Absence of the Book," Blanchot writes:

> Culture is linked to the book. The book as repository and receptacle of knowledge is identified with knowledge. The book is not only the book that sits in libraries—that labyrinth in which all combinations of forms, words, and letters are rolled up in volumes. The book is the Book. Still be to written, always already written, always paralysed by reading, the book constitutes the condition of every possibility of reading and writing.[7]

The preoccupation with the question of the book is not limited to French philosophers and their Anglo-American adherents. E. H. Curtius devoted a central chapter of his monumental study *European Literature and the Latin Middle Ages* to the history of the book as a symbol.[8] Tracing the image of the book from its inauspicious beginnings in ancient Greece to its apotheosis in Dante and the High Middle Ages, Curtius demonstrates how the book in figurative language not only represents different writers' regard for the medium of their art, but also reflects the changing way a culture regards itself and its own production. The optimism of, say, a Dante in believing that his own book can express the whole corpus of human knowledge is mirrored in the closing image of the *Divine Comedy*, in which the entirety of Creation and history reveals itself to be contained in a single book: "In the depth [of eternal Light], I saw contained, bound by love in one volume [*legato con amore in un volume*], that which is scattered in leaves through the universe" (*Paradise* XXXIII:85–88).[9] The book is that wherein the diversity of nature is unified into a single, all-encompassing structure.

At the beginning of the nineteenth century, Johann Wolfgang von Goethe observed the loss of the book as a viable symbol, and saw in this loss a symptom of cultural decay. In the *Maxims and Reflections* he laments that whereas in Shakespeare's time, the book was still able to be regarded as something sacred and therefore worthy of being used as a trope in poetic language, today "we put everything between covers [*Wir . . . broschieren jetzt alles*] and are hard pressed to respect either the bindings or the content."[10] The book, itself the primary receptacle of culture, can mirror in its physical form the spiritual state of that culture.

And yet, the vigor of a civilization cannot always be measured by how highly it values its books. Goethe himself, in a letter from 1769 to Friederike Oeser, juxtaposes bookish knowledge to knowledge acquired more freely through the confrontation with nature: "Upon simple paths I come to the knowledge of truth—often as far and further than others with all their library knowledge [*Bibliothekarwissenschaft*]."[11] To read from the Book of Nature is to reject the notion that knowledge is mediated only through human writing; it is to turn from the blind and belated culture of books to an unmediated source of truth. And yet the metaphor of nature as a "book" belies how the book, which must be read, has not only appropriated the whole sphere of culture as its province, but has subsumed the whole of nature as well.

As Gabriel Josipovici has shown for literature,[12] and as Hans Blumenberg has shown for philosophy and natural science,[13] the image of the book defines the way man has (or does not have) access to meaning in the world. It is not within the scope of this essay to consider the complex history of the metaphor of the book. It might, however, be helpful to indicate a few important stations in this history as a way of establishing a context for Klee's particular vision of the book.

1. Central to the Christian tradition from Augustine to Hugh of St. Victor and St. Bonaventure is the notion that God's creation consists of two books: the Book of Nature, or the universe, and *the* Book, or the Bible. After the Fall, human beings were unable to read the signs of nature, and so God wrote Scripture to replace this lost source of truth. If an individual assumes a proper attitude toward the world, however, he or she can regard nature itself as a scripture that is sufficiently meaningful. The world, like the Bible, is a sign left by its Creator which enables His noblest creation, the human being, to find its way back to grace.

2. The rise of modern science, enacted within the thought of Nicholas Cusanus, Copernicus, Galileo, and Kepler, is marked by a rejection of bookish learning in favor of an idea of the direct observation of nature.[14] Nature comes to be regarded as a perfectly legible text in which everything has its proper place, its beginning, middle, and end.[15]

3. The German romantics, most notably Novalis and Friedrich Schlegel, regarded the visible world as a hieroglyph or sign that, if properly deciphered, could lead the beholder to God. In *Die Lehrlinge zu Sais* from 1797, for example, Novalis writes how one may find in the forms of the physical world (forms which were then being discovered and explored by the natural sciences, with their own particular belief in the readability of the world) the key to a magical writing or *Wunderschrift*.[16] To read the deeper significance of the world's script, the sciences must combine with art to create a new *gnosis*.

4. Hegel appropriates the whole mystery of nature and its significance, subsuming it as one element among many that are to be enclosed in his own unfinished *Encyclopedia of the Philosophical Sciences*.[17] The *Encyclopedia* seeks not only to contain all organic and rational knowledge and to convey the

unity of this knowledge through the singularity of the book; it also aspires both to contain the knowable world in its structure, and, in accordance with its idea of totality, to give birth to itself.

5. Stéphane Mallarmé's "Book" or *Livre* claims to be, like the romantic encyclopedia, all-encompassing, but also acknowledges that, by definition, it can never come into being. The *Livre* represents an idea of a complete representation, *the* map of words as well as *the* mark of the mapmaker, around which all Mallarmé's literary efforts revolved, as around a fictional center.[18] His poems and prose works are fragments that, as he wrote to Verlaine, serve only to prove that this notional Book exists, "and . . . I have known what I have not been able to do."[19] Everything aspires to the condition of the *Livre:* "At bottom, you see, the world is made to end up as a beautiful book."[20]

It would be good here to recall Klee's words in his 1924 lecture to the Kunstverein in Jena:

> Sometimes I dream of a work on a vast scope, spanning all the way across element, object, content, and style. This is sure to remain a dream, a vague possibility. . . . We must go on looking for it. We have found parts, but not the whole.[21]

Klee's incomplete, uncompletable project, like Mallarmé's *Livre,* suggests an ideal of wholeness or totality that, while still haunting modernist art, exists only as a fiction against which actual works of art assume a fragmentary appearance. This notion of a totality outside of nature is founded on the mythic dimensions of the Book as it was formulated in Judeo-Christian theology and as it was appropriated by secular philosophy in the form of the encyclopedia. Now, however, the book cannot hold the Book. Dante's closing vision of *un volume* that is, in a sense, a vision of the closure of his own book, gives way to an idea of writing that always remains outside the book.[22] It is at this point that the metaphor of the book as something that can "contain" or embody knowledge reaches a crisis in its history; the book, as it were, can no longer be a *metaphor* at all. And if Goethe is right about the link between a culture and the way that culture can or cannot metaphorize its books, then the crisis expressed in Mallarmé's extravagant *Livre* will resound through Western culture's self-understanding.

Modern culture is haunted by a ghostly paradox in the image of the book. On one hand, the book no longer is capable of holding the totality which is its claim. The book becomes an object among other objects, mute and material. On the other hand, the book expands to become inescapable, creating a culture and a universe that cannot extricate itself from the tyranny of writing. Though engaged in an ongoing critique of the book, modern culture thinks of itself as being tragically embedded in the book. Far from being an object among objects, the book inscribes objects with its signature, so that where we thought there was nature, now there is only writing—a grim version of the Duke's happy words in Shakespeare's *As You Like It:* "And this our life . . . finds tongues in trees, books in the running brooks, sermons in the stones" (II, i, 15–17).

One form which modern meditations on the book has assumed is a tendency to stress the "thingness" of the book, as if by seeing the book in its "exterior deployment"[23] as object in the world one could measure its power and its limits. Mallarmé's *Coup de dés* destabilizes the notion that meaning is located "beyond" or outside of the presence of the text by creating a poem in which the material elements of writing—the paper and print—produce the effect of the poem in a new way. Like the rabbinical myth of the significance of the Torah written in white fire, the text of *Coup de dés* is suspended on the abyss ("l'Abime") of the white page which is as much or more of a significant "text" than are the printed words.[24] Perhaps the greatest example of a sustained confrontation with the question of writing in this century is James Joyce's *Finnegans Wake*. The punning, neologistic text of this massive work is always bringing into question the relationship between the printed page and the construction of meaning on the part of the reader. At one point in the book, a narrator with the voice of a scholar describes a certain manuscript (a parody of the *Wake* itself) that has been discovered in a junk heap outside of Dublin. Joyce illustrates the instability or errancy of the scholar's text by printing the acrobatics of the text's letters within the actual text of *Finnegans Wake:* the upside down and reverse *F*'s intrude on the written discourse of the scholar as he attempts to make out the manuscript's text. And yet the scholar desperately tries to separate his own writing from the wandering of the letter. He writes of the "eff," "aich," and "toppelfoul,"[25] as if to name the letter outright would be to admit that the text which talks "about" writing is itself writing, and therefore is also capable of errancy and subversion of its own authority. Thus in seeming to hide the materiality of writing, Joyce exposes the fabric of his text: the punning book of the *Wake* demonstrates in its own text a language always richer than knowledge, a language contained in the autonomy of the written sign.

The potential concreteness of writing has, in recent years, strayed out of the domain of literary language into the field of philosophy. Derrida carries out his critique of the "logocentrism" of Western thought by producing texts which call attention to their own material basis. In his "anti-book" entitled *Glas,* he juxtaposes on each page various texts by himself, Hegel, and Jean Genet, attempting thereby to show how philosophical texts (with Hegel symbolizing the culmination of a tradition stretching, as Franz Rosenzweig put it, from Ionia to Jena) are dependent on or trapped in the form of the book.[26]

In contemporary discourse on the question of the book, one arena of cultural practice has received rather little attention: namely, pictorial representations of the book in twentieth-century art.[27] The problem of how modern art does or does not come to grips with the book as symbol is, of course, a hugely complex phenomenon, one that involves, among other things, changing ideas about the so-called "sister arts" (poetry and painting) in this century, as well as the more general question of the relation between language and physical reality. One might want to ask, for example, whether a separation of the visual image from the culture of books is really asked for by the art of the twentieth century itself. The line, say, between the *Calligrammes* of Guillaume Apollinaire and the roughly contemporary poem-paintings from 1916 by Klee is thin indeed.[28] And yet it would be a mistake to simply regard this blurring of the boundaries between image and text as a fulfillment of the Horatian dictum *ut pictura poesis*. For Klee, at least, the book might represent the *idea* of readability and totality which haunts the image, yet the foundations of this idea are always already undercut by the material form in which the book becomes visible in the painting. What follows is an attempt to work out how, within five paintings by Klee, the book enters into the painting, and how thereby the word and the image are transformed.

III

As early as his 1914 painting *Teppich der Errinnerung (Carpet of Memory)*, Klee played with the possibility of including linguistic signs—letters, punctuation, etc.—in his compositions. In 1916 he produced a series of paintings which were themselves texts: a Chinese poem in translation, for example, would be "painted" in a manner that both rendered the text readable and illustrated the poem's content or mood. This project reached its most complex expression in Klee's 1918 watercolor entitled *Einst dem Grau der Nacht enttaucht . . . (Once Emerged from the Gray of Night)* now in Bern. In this small composition we see a work that is at once a book and a painting.

Einst dem Grau has a double structure (figure II). At the top of the painting, Klee has inscribed the text of the poem that within the painting he has composed in lines and colors. The inscription, written in black on white, frames the colorful painting, while the painting itself "contains" or frames the text of the inscription. Taken as a whole, Klee's poem-painting, a modern experiment in the *ut pictura poesis,* expresses the difficult, shifting relationship between image and poem, picture and book, as it were.[29] As beholders, we must engage in a double task: we must learn to "read" the painting as constitutive of a poem, and, more difficult, we must learn to still regard the poem as a painting, as a material thing with its own significant structure.

The painting itself is suitably *double* in its composition. It consists of two rectangular color planes separated by a silver strip of paper. Thus divided, the image forces us to shift our glance between the upper and lower sections. The silver strip resists our eye, causing our vision to glance off its shining surface like light on metal. Klee once wrote that "silver vibrates from dark to very light, and is also determined through movement. . . . Metallic values are remarkable pictorial medias."[30] The silver in *Einst dem Grau* sets our eye in motion between the two halves of the painting's double structure.

The two halves are formally alike. They consist of patches of color organized in neat, horizontal rows of equal widths. The horizontal rule remains always inviolable. Such strict horizontal organization has its "natural" model in the book or printed poem. Indeed this structure is echoed in the inscribed poem at the top of the sheet. Like a pupil writing in an exercise book, Klee has drawn faint lines to organize and contain his ordinary handwriting. The horizontal axis of the painting is further emphasized by the oblong format of the two rectangles and by the silver paper that separates them.

The horizontal rows are divided into colored squares which create a loose grid or checkerboard effect. Where there is no letter, the square has its own solid color. Wherever a letter appears framed in a square (every letter except the W is contained within a single square), the unity of color is broken. The lines that make up the letter mark off separate planes of different shapes, each of which can have its own color. Klee is not rigidly consistent in this matter: the upper and lower halves of the H, for example, and the left and right sides of the T are rendered in the same color, while each of the three planes marked off by the letter R has its own color. Nor are the same letters treated in the same way throughout: the B, for instance, is variously represented in two and three tones. And, of course, Klee is free to write each letter in whatever colors suits his purposes in that particular place in the composition. The principle of improvisation at work in *Einst dem Grau* may be a vehicle for Klee's expression, yet it threatens the readability of the poem-painting. In writing, the letters of the alphabet are legible insofar as they repeat and preserve the same recognizable shape. Klee lets his letters express themselves as individual, unique forms, as well as imitating the conventional shapes of the alphabet. The drama between text and image, expressed in that juxtaposition of the conventional writing at the top of the page and the poem-painting itself, is replayed in each letter of Klee's composition. Each written mark struggles between its re-presentational function as letter in a readable texts, and its expressive or presentational function as part of a pictorial image.[31] For when taken as a whole, the patches of color that constitute the poem create a structure on the level of the painting as a whole. The center of the top rectangle is dominated by warm tones (reds, oranges, and yellows) with cool colors collecting around the periphery. The lower rectangle is dominated by cool colors (greens and blues) spreading out from the center, with warm colors checkering the edges. There are, on the whole, more jarring color contrasts in the upper rectangle than in the lower, where the colors seem more ordered—due, perhaps, to the greater number of empty, solid squares there. If "read" from top to bottom, *Einst dem Grau* thus proceeds loosely through the spectrum: violet, red, orange, yellow, green, and blue. (It is interesting that Klee, in his own writings on the color wheel, makes the center of his "12-part [color] circle" the color gray; the "Grau" of the poem "Einst dem Grau . . ." and the silver of the dividing band of the painting itself may have reference to this organizing principle.) The improvisations around this basic structure serve often to balance the composition, as in the isolated red points around the C in the word "entschwebt" and in the few greens and blues in the center of the top rectangle.

In viewing the arrangement of colors in Klee's painting, we must let our gaze roam freely about the surface of the image, finding echoes and correspondences and discovering therein a pictorial structure. At the same time, by virtue of its being a poem as well as an image, *Einst dem Grau* has a predetermined structure laid down by the conventions of reading. To read the poem in Klee's painting, our eyes must make that familiar abecedarian journey from the left of the sheet to the right, proceeding in an orderly fashion through the painting. When viewed in this manner, the painting's overall structure becomes bound up with the movement and meaning of the poem. Here is the poem as it is written in the inscription at the top of the sheet:

> Einst dem Grau der Nacht enttaucht / Dann schwer und teuer / und stark vom Feuer / Abends voll von Gott und gebeugt // Nun ätherlings vom Blau umschauert, / entschwebt über Firner / zu klugen Gestirnen.

> [Once emerged from the gray of night / Then heavy and costly / and strong with fire / In the evening full of God and bent // Now towards heaven showered about with blue, / Carried away over the glacier / to the wise stars.]

The poem is divided into two parts, each with its own movement and temporality. Klee expresses this caesura pictorially by cutting the poem-painting in two just where the first series of three sentences or phrases ends and the second movement begins. It is interesting how in the poem, as it is modestly inscribed above the painting, Klee chooses not to put a period between sentences, using rather bars to denote verse lines and a double bar to signify the end of the movement. This casual notation takes on epic proportions in the two-edged bar of silver paper that divides the painting. The first lines of the poem move through three successive "moments," establishing the sense that the poem, and with it the painting, describes a process and a transformation. The three temporal qualifiers which begin each sentence or phrase— "Einst" [once], "Dann" [then], and "Abends" [in the evening]—posit a movement from beginning to middle to end. Because they lack both a subject and a verb, the phrases describe, for no specific subject at no specific time, a *pure process:* the passage of a day, the life of an individual or epoch, or what you will.

The painting embodies this process in its colors, taking advantage of hints within the poem. "Einst dem Grau/ der

Nacht / enttaucht" is painted suitably, in gray colors. Here
and there, lighter tones begin to appear, heralding the emer-
gence from darkness. Earlier we suggested how the letters in
Klee's composition break the otherwise solid color with their
lines. The letters of the opening words seem not only to
"represent" the coming of light as they speak of an *Ent-
tauchen* [emergence] from darkness, but in the way they
disturb the rhythm of the squares, they invoke light by break-
ing the monotony of their surroundings. Klee's painted words
have the power of the fiat, the divine *logos* that says, "Let
there be light" and there *is* light. The painting grows brighter
and warmer with the day, its light colors changing from pale
yellow to hectic red. In "Dann schwer/ und teuer/ und stark/
von Feuer," the middle of the day or life is marked mostly by
reds and oranges. With the coming of evening ("Abends / voll
von Gott") the tones become more subdued again.

In all these correspondences between word and image, the
possibility of overreading is always present, if not invited. The
word "Abends" has, for example, a dark *E* at its center which
we could easily read as a tonal analogy to the darkness of
night. What do we do, though, about the yellows in "Abend,"
or the greens and yellows in "Blau," for that matter? Perhaps
we must at present just go on cheerfully with our overreading,
hoping at least to see in our failed encounter with the image
the very caesura that Klee presents in his painting, that is, the
tension between word and picture, book and painting.

The second sentence of the poem begins with "Nun," a
temporal qualifier that lets the poem's drama unfold in the
now of its utterance. "Nun" plunges us into the absolute
present, making all that has gone before, that whole process
from "Einst" to "Abends," seem past or distant. The break
between the unspecified time in the first part of the poem
("Einst") and the deictic discourse that begins the second is
represented by the silver strip in Klee's composition, the "re-

markable" medium of representation that reflects and resists the gaze. The silver marks yet another opposition in the poem, for the threshold which we have crossed is that of death itself. "Nun ätherlings" represents, among other things, a movement into the present as transfiguration through death. Whatever is the real "subject" of the poem is now carried towards the wise stars. The various double structures in Klee's composition (e.g., word and image, written poem and poempainting, opposed rectangles of color above and below the silver bar, etc.) have a resonance *now*, a resonance in the relation of life to death.

It is interesting that the blue into which the subject of the poem soars is not something "outside" that is imagined as destination; rather, it is a presence that "covers" the subject: "Nun ätherlings / vom Blau umschauert." Klee's composition is itself "vom Blau umschauert," making the blue more present, more mysteriously substantial than it ever could be within a merely written book. Klee, that is, can write blue with blue.

The poem opens up to the sky and with it the painting becomes clearer, more open. Where in the top half of the painting every horizontal line had at least two words on it, two whole lines of the bottom rectangle are empty of writing. The painting aspires to the condition of pure, unbroken colors. How are we to read these wordless spaces? What meaning is grasped, what is heard when our eyes pass over the row of colors after the word "umschauert"? When we read a poem our eyes are paced, their movements structured in a particular tempo. To read Klee's painting as constitutive of a poem we must temper our vision to just such a rhythm. When we reach a wordless section of the painting, this rhythm is maintained despite the absence of written signs, and we find ourselves beholding the pure colors with the gaze of a reader, not a viewer. The book that we decipher, however, has become something palpable, something that engages our vision in its own exterior deployment as sign. Though empty of linguistic marks, the squares in Klee's painting become regarded as signs, pure signs which retain their signification only in the way they show themselves to an eye that is in the habit of reading. "The eye listens," wrote Paul Claudel, and if one pays attention one can hear sounds in Klee's colors. (Klee himself referred to his poem-paintings as "compositions" in the sense of a musician setting a poem to music.) The ä of "ätherlings," for example, expresses in its warm colors that are distinct from the surrounding values the shrill sound of the umlauted vowel. Indeed many of the open vowels appear as light in Klee's composition. Later, in his 1921 composition *Er küsse mich mit seines Mundes Kuss* [He kisses me with the kiss of his mouth] (figure 13), the vowels that would be stressed in reading this poem-painting of a verse from the Song of Songs are rendered in lighter tones. The poem's acoustic climax, the long drawn-out work "Öl" [oil] in the verse's final simile, is given strength by rendering the umlauted *O* in the warm orange that contrasts with the general gray tonality of the painting. And in this flame-like color, we are asked to sense both the sensuality of the biblical metaphor and the ignitable substance of the oil itself.

Here, though, we reach a difficulty. If it indeed is related expressively to the poem at all, is Klee's composition expressive of the poem's sound or its sense? Surely we might again be overreading if we say that the ä of "ätherlings" suggests a tone-color, while the blue of the rest of the word suggests the color of the "äther" [ether] itself. On what level does Klee ground the link between the poem and its visible presentation? I think it is appropriate that the poem itself expresses a similar aporia. Each of the two halves of the poem hang as qualifiers, as descriptions of a subject or action which are grammatically absent. What or who emerged from the gray only to arrive, in the evening, bent and full of God? What or who now travels in the blue towards the sky? The poem is a sphinx. It speaks a riddle which always breaks off, always borders on the very moment when the subject should take its place in the sentence. Perhaps Klee, in giving a living form to the poem, makes the picture itself, the book as image, stand in the place of the absent subject. As such, the painting does not really illustrate the poem, but expresses that which the poem leaves out as an unfinished sentence. The painting literally fills the absence of the book.

And indeed, from a formal perspective, this is precisely what is happening in *Einst dem Grau*. The colors of Klee's composition take place where the letters are not. They fill the gaps between signs and between the parts of signs. In Klee's terms, the written letters are active lines that, within the painting, become passive edges of colored planes.[32] The radical outcome of this technique of filling the spaces left by the letters is that the text becomes itself illegible in places. How can we tell the difference between one of Klee's *L*'s, as in the word "voll," from an empty space? How can we know whether a certain letter is an *H* or an *E* except by its semantic context? Such gaps in the text are precisely what necessitate the more conventional inscription of the poem at the top of Klee's picture. Words such as "zu" and "klugen" are only readable because we already know what they must be. Klee understood that this practice of sometimes distinguishing, through color contrasts, planes marked off by the lines of letters, while at other times rendering certain planes in the same color as their adjacent plane, would create a text that is difficult to read. In the *Notebooks* he specifically states that "Where planar units meet in a line a change of element [by which he means color, tone, or material] is necesssary."[33]

Klee writes his poem-painting *sous rature*, as it were, under the erasure of pure color. His meditation on the relationship of a text to its material support is linked to all those twentieth-century experiments in the form of the book that we have mentioned, from the *Coup de dés* of Mallarmé and the picture-poems of Christian Morgenstern to Joyce's *Finnegans Wake*. What is at stake is the play between the sensible and the intelligible, between materiality and ideality. It is important that the painting goes beyond the text in the completion of its structure, resting as it does on those rhythmical squares of color in the bottom line which now have been invested with the meaning and space of the stars. Yet to reach this extravagant stage of signification it was necessary that the painting once descend and be touched by the book.

Klee represents the book, or creates a painting which *is* a book, only to show the book's limits. As in *Zeichen in Gelb*, the painting *Einst dem Grau* is there exactly where the poem (the lines of the letters) is not. Though it seems to illustrate the text, invoking colors and contrasts that are proper to the poem's constative message, the painting makes present exactly what was missing in the poem: the subject and the verb of the action. It is part of Klee's genius that *Einst dem Grau* should, along with all other levels of signification, also sustain a more conventional illustration of the poem. For when taken as a pictorial whole, Klee's composition does conjure up the world as described by the poem: the sun, radiating at the "horizon" from the center of the upper rectangle's lower edge, is reflected on the ice-covered earth that is the lower rectangle. And the silver strip at the center is the horizon, the invisible threshold between heaven and earth.

The "illustrative" aspect of Klee's painting is, however, more of a *coup de grâce* than the true center of his artistic intentions. In this painting-book the artist has both invoked the notion of images at the service of texts, and asserted the autonomy of the visual sign. In a passage by Robert Delauney which Klee translated for *Der Sturm* in 1913, we read that the movement beyond the object in art is linked to a movement

FIGURE 13. Paul Klee, *Let Him Kiss Me with the Kiss of His Mouth* (1921).
Watercolor over pen and India ink and pencil on paper, 16.1×23 cm.
Lucerne, Angela Rosengart Collection (1921.142). © 1990, copyright by
COSMOPRESS, Geneva.

FIGURE 14. Paul Klee,
Document (1933).
Oil, watercolor, and plaster
on gauze and wood,
22.8×19.1 cm. Lucerne,
Angela Rosengart Collec-
tion (1933.Z.3). © 1990,
copyright by COSMO-
PRESS, Geneva.

FIGURE 15. Paul Klee, *Plant Script Picture* (1932).
Watercolor on colored sheet, 25.2 × 52.3 cm. Bern Kunstmuseum, Paul Klee
Foundation (1932.61). © 1989, copyright by COSMOPRESS, Geneva.

FIGURE 17. Caspar David Friedrich, *Cemetery in the Snow* (1827).
Oil on canvas, 31 × 25.3 cm. Leipzig, Museum der bildenden Künst.

FIGURE 18. Caspar David Friedrich, *View from the Studio of the Artist, Right Window* (1805/6).
Pencil and sepia, 31 × 24 cm. Vienna, Kunsthistorisches Museum.

FIGURE 19. Paul Klee, *Open Book* (1930).
Gouache over white lacquer on canvas, 45.5 × 42.5 cm. New York, Guggenheim Museum. Photo: David Heald. © 1990, copyright by COSMOPRESS, Geneva.

FIGURE 20. Paul Klee, *Aquarium with Silvery-Blue Fishes* (1924).
Ink and wash, 22.5 × 12.1 cm. Bern, private collection. © 1990, copyright
by COSMOPRESS, Geneva.

FIGURE 21. Paul Klee, illustrations from *Notebooks*, I:52, of "endotopic" and "exotopic" treatment of the plane.
© 1990, copyright by COSMOPRESS, Geneva.

FIGURE 22. Paul Klee, *Open* (1933).
Watercolor and wax, muslin on wood, 40.7 × 55 cm. Bern, Felix Klee Collection (1933.A6.306). © 1989, copyright by COSMOPRESS, Geneva.

FIGURE 23. Paul Klee, *Legend of the Nile* (1937). Pastel on cotton on burlap, 69×61 cm. Bern, Kunstmuseum, Hermann and Margrit Rupf-Stiftun (1937.215). © 1989, copyright by COSMOPRESS, Geneva.

beyond the book: "As long as art does not free itself from the object, it remains description, literature; it lowers itself in the use of imperfect means of expression and damns itself to the slavery of imitation."[34] This statement, fundamental for an understanding of twentieth-century art and the rise of abstraction, suggests that it is precisely against literariness, against the culture of the book that the visual image must create its images. It is perhaps not coincidental that the "end" of the book in *Einst dem Grau* is that series of squares of undisturbed color. They prefigure one of Klee's most radical departures from the art of the Occident: his series of "magic squares" that were done throughout the years between 1923 and 1937.[35] In these compositions, which Will Grohmann places at the "innermost circle" of the artist's oeuvre, we see painting at its furthest remove from any narrative or illustrative elements, and yet the grid that makes up *Einst dem Grau* suggests that what might now be abstract once ("einst") was more bookish.

IV

In *Einst dem Grau* the painting is a kind of book. What happens, though, when Klee represents the book as an object *within* the painting? In Klee's 1933 composition entitled *Urkunde (Document)* (figure 14), now in the Angela Rosengart Collection in Lucerne, the artist has placed a brownish-white rectangle, vertical in format, exactly in the center of the composition. The vertical edges are rough, and in the way they are accented unevenly in brown, they give the impression of casting a shadow in the pinkish background. The rectangle thus looks as if it were a separate thing pasted on to the composition: a piece of papyrus, carefully centered, there for us to inspect. The brown colors are signs of the page's antiquity, and the gauze-like texture of the rest of *Urkunde* suggests the actual fabric of papyrus. Covering the rectangle and written in the same brown that renders the edges of the "papyrus" are cryptic signs arranged like writing in horizontal rows. Although certain of their hieroglyphs resemble known signs (e.g., one can make out *O*'s, *F*'s, *H*'s, deltas, as well as certain mathematical symbols like the equals sign and the sign of congruence), the writing is of an unknown or fictional alphabet. Like an inscription in a lost language for which we have no Rosetta Stone, Klee's signs in *Urkunde* are impossible to read, yet recognizable *as writing*. They cannot be mistaken for "mere" decoration.

One language, though, that we can read in Klee's painting is the cultural language of things-on-display, or objects that are privileged for our gaze in the manner of an exhibition or *ostensio*. Klee places the "document" at the center of his composition and frames it with a pinkish border that acts like a matt and with two strips of brownish-white (the same color as the "document" itself) that form the right and left borders of the painting. Klee presents his cryptic writing to us with the straightforward symmetry and understated color of a museum display. Just as the document seems spatially separate from the rest of the painting by the *tableau objet* character of the white rectangle fringed in brown (i.e., it seems pasted to the painting as a separate thing), the invocation of the language of the museum distances the object from us temporally, as well. The document becomes now an artifact designated for our inspection because of the value that age or rareness has given it. Both acts of distancing or framing, the trompe l'oeil aspect and the language of the museum, also sustain the document's materiality, its thingness. It is something on display, something which has survived intact as an object and is therefore worthy of display and study. This emphasis on the materiality of what Klee puts before us is not, of course, specific to the painting *Urkunde*; Klee's general tendency to display the edges of the pieces of paper, canvas, or fabric

upon which he works suggests always an insistence on show-
ing the material basis of his art. What, though, is on display
in *Urkunde?*

The word "Urkunde" is compounded from the prefix *ur-*,
which means "original" or primal, or stresses the word with
which it is linked, and *kunde* which means "information,"
"knowledge," or "science" (as in, say, "Pflanzenkunde"). An
urkunde can be anything that mediates human thought, from
an inscription or piece of writing to a proof of ownership or
academic degree. The Magna Carta is an *urkunde* as is the
certificate of excellence that hangs above the cashier's desk
in a family restaurant. Thus at its loftiest and most general
level, an *urkunde* is a written document, a book whose "mes-
sage" is unreadable. Instead of mediating a particular thought
or proclamation, it documents writing itself in its primary or
original state. There is something ironic about this display of
the book as primal object or epistemological mediation. For
at the lower left of the rectangle, written in the same brown
as the rest of the inscription is Paul Klee's own signature. Like
the forger's nightmare of dating his fake work, "Made in 2000
B.C.," Klee's signature, present not at the corner of the whole
composition, but within the *urkunde* itself is an anachronism
that calls the "originality" of the document in question. The
signature acts at once like a proof of the document's authen-
ticity (as one signs an official document), and as a writing that
brings the "truth" of the *urkunde*—that primal knowledge
sustained by writing—into question.

Unless, of course, the *urkunde* is a document of Klee's
writing, preserved and displayed for posterity to see. At the
opening of his discussion of active, passive, and medial lines
in the *Notebooks,* Klee writes: "For the present let us content
ourselves with the most primitive of elements, the line. At the
dawn of civilization, *when writing and drawing were the
same thing,* it was the basic element." (italics added)[36] It is

interesting that we should find such a statement written within a text like that of the *Notebooks*. Klee's "book" itself (re)establishes a kind of primal unity between analytic drawing and descriptive or ecphrastic writing. And yet, helpful as it is, Klee's vision of the original equivalence of drawing and writing is a fiction: as soon as writing is regarded *as* writing, as soon as the first person who ever wrote or inscribed a "sign" on a stone that was to be "read" as document of something else, as soon as this happens and the fundamental shift between vision and seeing constitutive in writing is enacted, then drawing (the interest in the line as line) vanishes into the absence that is writing. *Urkunde* represents a kind of reappropriation of that fictional unity. It presents us with a writing which, because it is unreadable, has become purely a sign (divorced from the otherness that meaning could give it) and thus is equivalent to drawing. *Urkunde* documents Klee's primal scene of writing-as-drawing, the pure exteriority of the book. As Maurice Blanchot would say, such a script is "writing outside of language, writing which would be in some sense originally language making it impossible for there to be any object (present or absent) of language."[37] The theme of an indecipherable writing or a lost or unreadable document haunts modern literature. In Kafka's *The Castle*, for example, letters and documents are constantly being misplaced or fail to reach their destination. Their failure to mediate a message, to find their proper reader, mirrors the effect of Kafka's novel itself which, as a book, is incomplete and uncompletable and which, like the novel's hero K., can only circumscribe but never attain full significance. In *The Trial*, too, the Law rests in a book (the parable of the *Türhütter*) which is at once binding in its significance and impossible to interpret: "Die Schrift is unveränderlich, und die Meinungen [the interpretations it engenders] sind oft nur ein Ausdruck der Verzweiflung darüber. [The text is unalterable, and the opinions about it

are often only an expression of despair about this.]"[38] Joyce's
Finnegans Wake has as its thematic center a lost or unreada-
ble text, as well. The "plot" of the novel, the true story about
the guilt or innocence of the hero, is contained in a letter (or
"litter" as Joyce puns it) which was lost in a dump yard, and
when it is retrieved, it is a torn and unreadable text, a "protei-
form . . . polyhedron of scripture."[39] At one point, the narra-
tor asks us to "stoop if [we] are abecedminded, to this claybed
[i.e., to the clay tablet that is the lost letter/book]" and ob-
serve its writing: "A middenhide hoard of objects! Olives,
beets, kimmells, dollies, alfrids, beatties, cormaks, and dal-
tons."[40] The "objects" which we see are not only roots, fruits,
etc., but in their *sounds* as words, they echo the letters of
both the Hebrew and the Greek alphabets: the Hebrew alpha-
bet begins with aleph, beth, daleth, and the Greek with alpha,
beta, gamma, and delta. Language is, following Joyce's guid-
ing philosopher, Vico, grounded in the arbitrary *objet-trouvé*.
Letters, the raw material of the book, are returned to the inert
thingness of objects. And in this giving over of writing to
nature, Joyce uncovers the materiality of his own book.

In Klee's oeuvre, we find a striking parallel to Joyce's
"middenhide" ("midden" as prehistoric junkheap + "hide"
as the concealing and revealing fabric of language) in the
painting of *Pflanzenschriftbild* of 1931 (figure 15). Against a
dark brown ground, Klee has painted the figures in various
sizes, shapes, and colors. The title announces that what we
see is a picture of plant-writing. The colored forms, in which
we can "read" such letters as *t, u, v, w, y,* and *z,* as well as
forms reminiscent of Arabic script, Klee recalls the notion of
the "natural" signature of the world present in Novalis and
explicit in the just-quoted passage from Joyce, where olives
are alephs and beets are beths. The brown background of
Klee's composition is literally *ground* itself—the earth or soil
out of which the sign-plants are growing. Of course, the

presence of an "alphabet" in Joyce's and Klee's "books" remains only a surmise. The forms, written and painted, do not give their significance unambiguously to the interpreter. To *see* a *y* or a *w* in the colored shapes in Klee's painting, or to *hear* the letter "aleph" in the word "olive" in Joyce, is to discern the relationship between writing as material thing and its potential to signify something else.

What is important in these examples is not just the "theme" of the book in works of art in this century. The book, whenever it is invoked, deconstructs the very discourse or image which invokes it. The undecipherable "litter" unearthed in *Finnegans Wake* becomes, when written about in Joyce's own partly decipherable book, a synecdoche for the artist's work as a whole. Similarly, Klee's *Urkunde* situates Klee's art (as it is "documented" in the signature at the lower right corner of the written text) at an aporia between writing and drawing, between the book and pure painting.

V

Let us look more closely at Paul Klee's signs. Near the center of Klee's *Composition with Windows* a sign that seems to be an exclamation point has started to bud (figure 16). What surprise does it register? What statement or exclamation does it announce? Perhaps only surprise that the sign itself is turning into a plant: on the top of the figure and off to both sides, groups of three leaves are sprouting clones of the exclamation point's shape. The dot below this lush signifier remains inert, but takes on the character of a bulb or root. The inert literality of linguistic signs has become, as it were, naturalized. The written mark, that is, has taken on a life of its own and installed itself in the landscape as a thing among things. What is more surprising is that Klee does not provide a landscape in which the exclamation point/plant can be surprised. The painting is called *Composition with Windows* *(Komposition mit Fenstern)* and we struggle to find the windows thus named. What we do find are many cross-like designs within squares, often with two diagonal lines cutting the upper left and right corners of the square. The image looks schematic, like a child's drawing of a window with curtains drawn aside. The windows in Klee's composition have endured the opposite fate from that of the exclamation point. They, the "real-world" subject of the painting, have become schematized, sterilized into conventional signifiers. No wonder the painting is surprised! Conventional signs have returned to nature, while real things are becoming signs.

The lines that form the "windows" play a role in structuring Klee's painting. In general, *Composition with Windows* is organized around a network of lines that run vertically and horizontally across the canvas; in their intersection, they close off rectangular planes of color which vary in size, color, and density of tone. The patchwork of colored squares is most concentrated at the center. Each is rendered in a distinct tone —red, white, black, and brown—which sets it off against its neighbor. Elsewhere on the canvas Klee creates a pattern of rectangles with different means: at the upper right, for example, white lines—which we have encountered in their function as depicting windows—divide the large patch of red into four or more smaller squares. Where the central planes of color were distinguished from one another by their distinctive color, here Klee "draws" boundaries on a solid plane by using a white line. (Glaesemer has used Klee's own notion of active, medial, and passive lines to explain these different effects.)[41] Actual lines and the lines implied by the edges of planes act together dialectically to create the structure of the composition. The network of horizontals and verticals is not rigid, but bends and curves in various places. The composition takes on an aspect like a patchwork cloth that has not been smoothed flush with the picture plane, but has waves and raised spots. These distortions give the painting a sense of depth. In addition, other forms play about the composition. The black arch shape just right of center, in the negative of an arch to the right of the exclamation point and in the two semicircles that make up the letter *B,* is echoed by the curving pattern of brush strokes and lines at the top of the painting. The movement that circulates through the strong white diagonal rises up to the right of the lower frame. This diagonal is echoed throughout the painting by all those white lines which indicate the "curtain" in the window, as well as by the diagonally sprouting buds of the exclamation point and the branches of the schematic tree at the lower right.

Klee unifies his composition through his use of color as well as line. Dark red, black, brown, and white dominate the painting while shades of blue, green, and purple play here and there over the surface. Each color serves a particular function. Black renders the peculiar "signs" which appear in the composition (the *B,* exclamation point, the delta, etc.) as well as a few of the smaller planes near the very concentrated center. Red appears either in well-defined planes or else, more often, it is spread out over larger surfaces which are themselves divided into smaller squares. Brown appears as a kind of ground tone that ties the composition together. And the pale blues, purples, and greens punctuate the composition rather like washes of color. Klee uses white in a very complex manner. Rather than being a highlight that emphasizes the solidity of particular planes, white appears within colored planes as a place where light seems to *shine through.* "Solid" forms are represented in single, solid colors (e.g., the central squares) while squares with white on them (as in the area at the center of the lower portion of the painting) appear transparent. Chiaroscuro, shading from dark to light, has just the opposite effect in Klee's composition than its use in traditional pictorial representation.[42] Things modeled in light and shadow appear thinner and less solid than flat surfaces of color. In *Composition with Windows* the white acts as if it were light shining through a window wherever the color has been wiped away.

This is because Klee's *Composition with Windows* is itself like a window or stained glass which seems to let light through its colored surface. The white acts as if it marks a point where color is thin or has been wiped away so that the light can shine through to us *from behind the picture plane.* How strange, then, that the window itself—whose schematized squares with crosses in them—should be rendered in white lines. That which is opaque and solid in real windows becomes transparent in Klee. That is, the frame and lattice represented in white in *Composition with Windows* seems to let light in while the glass itself keeps light out.

Conventional signs have become natural objects in Klee's painting (the exclamation point), while real objects (the window) have been reduced to mere signs. And these signs, in turn, operate in just the opposite manner as their natural model. The sign for the window is transparent where it should be solid, invisible where it should be visible. What, then, do we see in Klee's window?

In a sense, the abstract composition of Klee's painting can be read to constitute a "landscape." In what would then be the foreground, a very schematized flower rises from what could be construed as either the landscape's ground or a windowsill. Higher up and to the right are two trees, one drawn as a single line with diagonal branches growing out from either side, the other rendered as a sort of y shape with small dots for leaves. These two figures represent either two different species of trees, or two distinct conventions for representing trees. The sense of the landscape as a catalog of signs becomes clearer in the various cryptograms scattered about the painting: the *B* with an equals sign; the curious quasi-mathematical delta with a point under it; at the right of center, the *X* with a horizontal line running through it, etc. The arch-shaped top of the composition organizes the picture into a narrowing structure which lets the "landscape" be read as if it receded into space. Indeed I can see another kind of scene in Klee's composition. The crosses, which I have hitherto identified as window-lattices, form, if read as crosses in space, a picture of a cemetery with Christian grave markers receding into the distance. The diagonal lines of the "curtains," within this reading of things, would then become the roof of the cross—a design of grave markers common in Austria, Germany, and Switzerland. Klee's composition becomes a cemetery with distinct echoes of the romantic graveyard tradition such as we see in the paintings of Caspar David Friedrich (figure 17).

Ghosts of the romantic tradition are present in the central subject matter of Klee's *Composition with Windows,* as well. The open window, with its suggestion of a longing for nature and for the infinite, is one of romantic painting's favorite visual emblems (figure 18).[43] We need not stop with Friedrich in tracing Klee's ancestry, however, for since the Renaissance Western painting has been metaphorized as the transformation of the flat surface of the canvas into a *window* onto the world. Already in the fifteenth century Alberti called painting a "kind of window"; and Albrecht Dürer, in translating the Latin word *perspectiva* as "Durchsehung" (a seeing-through something), regards the picture plane as something through which one looks.[44] Klee turns this whole tradition of representation on its head. We do not see through *Composition with Windows* as through a window, but rather we see flat, transparent *signs* of windows which let light in exactly where they should frame the hallowed illusionistic "space" of the painted image. Illusionism, the painting-as-window, appears here as mere convention and in the place of the naturalistic panorama, arbitrary signs have taken root as the solid inhabitants of a visible world. The window, that mediator between nature and culture, between the closed dwelling place of man and the endless prospect of the universe, has thus revealed quite a different prospect. The mimetic depiction of nature in the form of landscape or view, becomes here a cultural construction, a conventional sign, while the clearly arbitrary signifiers (the letter, mathematical symbol, written mark of punctuation, etc.), endowed with an uncanny materiality, seem filled with the life of nature. To say that Klee reduces the painting to conventional signs would be wrong, for these signs, freed from their bondage to a purely representational function, stalk about the landscape with as little codified meaning and as much life as beasts in a forest.

VI

Up until now we have discussed the image of the book in a very broad sense, as encompassing any reference to the materiality of writing. Let us now examine Klee's most explicit invocation of the book in his 1933 painting *Offenes Buch* [*Open Book*] now in the Guggenheim Museum (figure 19). The painting is composed of a series of overlapping planes that recall, generally, the pages of a book as they cover, fold over, or stand at an angle to one another. Each plane is distinguished from the one "behind" it through cross-hatchings that radiate outward from the pages' edges creating a shadow on the surface behind. The volume or thickness of the book is indicated, synecdochically, as it were, by that dark brown vertical rectangle at the right of the composition that runs parallel to the picture's frame. Less like a mimetic rendering of a book from a certain angle, Klee's *Offenes Buch* assembles *signs* of the object's qualities. Thus the dark strip indicating volume is juxtaposed to the image of flat, overlapping planes as two alternative modes of representing the book as object.

The planes themselves, set off against one another by the hatchings, themselves create a sense of depth in the composition. This technique of overlapping and paradoxically volumetric planes has precedents within Klee's oeuvre, for example in the 1924 *Aquarium with Silvery Blue Fishes* (figure 20). In his *Notebooks* Klee explains the need for such a device for creating a sense of depth when the convention of perspective is abandoned. Through the use of what the artist calls "endotopic" and "exotopic" treatments of surfaces, in which modeling or cross-hatching radiates either inward or outward from the edges of the planes, the eye, drawn from a lighter point to a darker outer space, is given a sense of movement from inside to out, fore to rear (plate 21).[45] In the *Open Book,* the "exotopic" hatching lets the central planes appear raised towards us at the same time as they effect a movement from the center toward the edges of the composition. The book, engaged in a movement which seems to grow from the center, is opening for our gaze.

The arrangement of overlapping planes at various angles to one another becomes in Klee a "sign" of openness itself. In the painting entitled *Offen* from 1933, in the Felix Klee Collection, we have a similar effect of book or door-like structures standing at various angles to the picture plane (figure 22). At the same time, though, Klee's *Open Book* seems to be "closing" inward toward the center. The pages do not grow smaller as they become more distant from our eye (as they would in conventional perspective). Like boxes in boxes or mirrors in mirrors, the pages of the book shrink as they reach the center, that is, as they display to our reading eye that page to which the book is opened. Each plane contains the plane which is "in front" of it within its boundaries until, at the very center, we reach that peculiar triangle with eleven small squares inscribed on it. It is as if the foreground (rather than the horizon) were the painting's vanishing point. Our eye travels into the open book as if into an infinite regression. How can we read this Piranese-like prison book?

The title of the painting, *Offenes Buch* or *Open Book,* is a *mot* for readability. For something to be an "open book" its meaning or intention must be immediately accessible to the beholder. When I say, "Er las in ihrem Gesicht wie in einem offenen Buch [He read in her face as in an open book]," then I am invoking the image of the book to denote a situation of the complete transparency of signification. What we find in Klee's book, though, are only more books. At the center of the composition we discover, instead of writing, that group of tiny squares which repeat the rectangular structure of a book. It is as if the book contained only itself transformed into a sign, as if at the "center" of the book there were only more books. The sign of the book, the empty squares which are inscribed in Klee's book, have replaced writing or meaning as that which is "contained" in the open book. It is interesting that, according to the conventions of perspective, the central group of four planes offset by the black area around its left side, creates just the opposite effect of an opening book. That dark black which, so prominent in the composition, could represent either the shadow cast by the front "page," or the page behind, is larger than the page which would be in front of it. The *Open Book* would thus seem to be closing at its center. Unless, of course, the central group of four planes is read as opening up *behind* the picture plane onto a darkness represented by that black surface. The book opens up to nothingness, Mallarmé's "l'Abîme." Jacques Derrida, in his essay "Ellipses," writes of the emptiness of the book in the book:

> The center of the first book should not have been repeatable in its own representation. Once it lends itself a single time to such a representation—that is, once it is written—when one can read a book in the book, a center in the center, an origin in the origin, it is the abyss, is the bottomlessness of infinite redoubling.[46]

Klee's painting *Offenes Buch* displays the book emptied of the signs that would take us beyond the book. Instead of containing something, the book opens onto the abyss of its own self-representation. What it leaves behind is only its material structure (the planes of the pages and the lines that they describe) which organizes Klee's own composition. This is a common strategy in Klee's art: to take an object laden with cultural or symbolic significance (as, say, the book, the window, or the grave), and employ it as a mere structuring element in the painting. And though he pretends to erase history from his symbols, their traditional content always haunts them still. The abyss sustained by Klee's *Open Book* is not merely the appropriation of the symbol of the book as, willy-nilly, a vehicle for an abstract construction of empty forms. The abyss of the book expresses the crisis of the culture of writing in this century.

VII

Klee's art returns again and again to the theme of writing and the book, sometimes to empty the book of its privileged cultural significance, sometimes to fill his paintings with the mere referential *energy* of writing. In his paintings from 1937 on, Klee becomes increasingly interested in the formal and

symbolic potentials of representing bold graphic signs, mod-
eled often after Arabic script or Egyptian hieroglyphs, that
delimit and structure flat planes of color—a formula which
we see in *Yellow Signs* of 1937. In *The Legend of the Nile* of
the same year, the artist arranges various orange-brown signs
on a field of blue and gray rectangular planes (figure 23). The
title suggests that the painting "tells a story" from the world
of the Nile and therefore of great antiquity. What the story
says we do not know for we have no Rosetta Stone with
which to translate its symbols. We can, however, make out at
least one story in Klee's painting: the legend of the origin of
writing itself. The signs that appear in the painting span the
whole evolution of the linguistic symbol. We see the picto-
graph (like the "fish" at the lower left or the "boat" with
oarsmen and a standing passenger) that refers to its meaning
simply by imitating in its form the object represented. We
also see various abbreviated or abstracted forms of pictures
which, according to some accounts, were the origins of the
modern alphabet and which refer synecdochically to their
reference, as in the shape reminiscent of a ship's prow which
could signify "boat" at the lower left. And finally, we have
letters of the Greek and Roman alphabets proper: the pi and
gamma as well as the *x, y, u,* etc.

What can also emerge in Klee's painting is the pictorial
setting for this legend of the book: the boat rides over a
"water" in which a fish swims under a sun (that pink circle at
the upper left). The fact that we can read the scene in this
way is revealed to be as much a function of signification, and
therefore of writing at its origins, as any legend which might
be inscribed in a scroll or book. The blue squares are given
significance as sky and water because they are interpreted by
both the work's title and by those other written pictographs
which, assembled on the canvas, together create a sign for
space itself. What we read in this tale is the story Klee tells

again and again in his artistic career: the legend of painting bound up inextricably with the book.

One final note on the purpose and scope of this essay. I have tried to do two things in my reading of Paul Klee and his engagement with the book (or written text) as an image. First, I have located the discussion of the artist's work within literary critical discourses about writing and the book. While this does not exclude an approach to the artist's oeuvre from the perspective of its relation to other *painters* of his time working along similar lines, it provides a useful reduction for evaluating the very new conception of art as it is formulated explicitly and implicitly by Klee—a conception, moreover, that specifically refuses to separate written language from visual image in as strict a manner as does the discipline of art history itself. Second, I have tried to suggest the areas in Klee's pictorial work that are most open to such an analysis. In this regard, I have barely touched on the most obvious area of Klee's output as a visual thinker, as it were. A sustained reading of the book in Klee would have to address the question of Klee's own writing (the *Notebooks* and even the diaries) and the implications of this tendency to analyze his art in light of the culture of writing. Such a study would, I think, be an important contribution not only to the understanding of Klee, but also for the question of twentieth-century art's supposed emancipation from illustration and the culture of the book.

NOTES

1. Paul Klee, *Notebooks. Volume I: The Thinking Eye,* edited by Jürg Spiller, translated by Ralph Manheim (London: Lund Humphries, 1961), p. 453.
2. Ibid., I: 291.

3. For the interruptive character of writing, see Jacques Derrida, "Edmund Jabès and the Question of the Book," in *Writing and Difference*, translated by Alan Bass (London: Routledge & Kegan Paul, 1978), pp. 70–72.

4. See Gershom Scholem, *Kabbalah* (New York: Quadrangle Books, 1974), p. 174. While it is not important whether Klee actually knew of this legend, he may have encountered it in Martin Buber's very popular *Legende des Ballschem,* published in 1907. For Buber's position in German culture of the time, see Scholem, "Martin Bubers Auffassung des Judentums" in *Judaica* (Frankfurt: Suhrkamp Verlag, 1970), II: 133–92.

5. For the question of "ground," see Martin Heidegger, "Vom Wesen des Grundes," in *Wegmarken*, 2d ed. (Frankfurt: Vittorio Klostermann, 1978), pp. 123–73; see also Geoffrey H. Hartman, *Saving the Text: Literature/Derrida/Philosophy* (Baltimore: Johns Hopkins University Press, 1981), pp. 64–66.

6. For the form assumed by Derrida's books, see Hartman, *Saving the Text.*

7. Maurice Blanchot, "The Absence of the Book," originally published in *L'Entretien infini* (1969), translated in *The Gaze of Orpheus and Other Literary Essays,* translated by Lydia David (Barrytown, N.Y.: Station Hill Press, 1981), p. 146.

8. Ernst Robert Curtius, *European Literature and the Latin Middle Ages,* translated by Willard Trask (Princeton, N.J.: Princeton University Press, 1973), pp. 303–38.

9. Dante, *The Divine Comedy,* translated by John D. Sinclair (New York: Oxford University Press, 1939).

10. Johann Wolfgang von Goethe, *Werke,* edited by Ernst Beutler (Zurich: Artemis Verlag, 1949), 9: 523, as cited in Curtius, *European Literature,* p. 303.

11. Goethe to Friederike Oeser, February 13, 1769, in *Werke,* 18: 121.

12. Gabrieli Josipovici, *The World and the Book: A Study of Modern Fiction,* 2d ed. (London: Macmillan, 1979), pp. 25–51, 286–311.

13. Hans Blumenberg, *Die Lesbarkeit der Welt* (Frankfurt: Suhrkamp Verlag, 1981).

14. For the role of Nicholas of Cusa in establishing and legitimating a "method" for the natural sciences as distinct from the reading of biblical texts, see Hans Blumenberg, *Die Legitimität der Neuzeit. 4. Aspekte der Epochenschwelle: Cusaner und Nolaner,* 2d ed. (Frankfurt: Suhrkamp Verlag, 1982), pp. 34–108; for Copernicus, see Blumenberg, *Die Genesis der kopernikanischen Welt,* 3 vols. (Frankfurt: Suhrkamp Verlag, 1981).

15. For the relationship between the image of the book and a notion of closure, see Frank Kermode, *The Sense of an Ending: Studies in the Theory of Fiction* (London: Oxford University Press, 1966), pp. 3–89.

16. Friedrich von Hardenberg [Novalis], *Die Lehrlinge zu Sais, Gedichte, und Fragmente,* edited by Martin Kiessig (Stuttgart: Reclam, 1975), p. 3.

17. For an important discussion of the claims of Hegel's *Encyclopedia,* see Jacques Derrida, "Outwork, prefacing," in *Dissemination,* translated by Barbara Johnson (Chicago: University of Chicago Press, 1981), p. 47ff.

18. Judy Kravis, *The Prose of Mallarmé: The Evolution of Literary Language* (Cambridge: Cambridge University Press, 1976), pp. 179–80.

19. Stéphane Mallarmé, *Oeuvres complète* (Paris: Gallimard, 1945), p. 663.

20. Ibid.

21. Klee, *Notebooks* I: 95.

22. For the notion of "writing outside the book," see Blanchot, "The Absence of the Book," p. 151.

23. I take this term from Michel Foucault's reading of Saussure's emphasis on the acoustic quality of the signifier, in "What is an Author?," in *Language, Counter-Memory, Practice: Selected Essays and Interviews,* edited and translated by Donald F. Bouchard and Sherry Simon (Ithaca: Cornell University Press, 1977), p. 116.

24. Stéphane Mallarmé, *Poem, Un Coup de dés jamais n'abolira le hazard,* facsimile ed. (Geneva: D'Albert Kundig, 1943), p. 3a.

25. James Joyce, *Finnegans Wake* (New York: Viking, 1958), pp. 120–21.

26. Jacques Derrida, *Glas* (Paris: Editions Galileé, 1975).

27. For a brief survey of the image of the book in Western art, see Jan Bialostocki, *Bücher der Weisheit oder Bücher der Vergangenheit. Zur Symbolik des Buches in der Kunst* (Heidelberg: Abhandlungen der Heidelberger Akademie der Wissenschaft, Philosophisch-historische Klasse, 1984), 5.

28. See Ann Temkin's discussion of the conjunction of painting and poetry in her essay, "Klee and the Avant-Garde 1912–1940" in the exhibition catalog of *Paul Klee,* edited by Carolyn Lanchner (New York: Museum of Modern Art, 1987), p. 17.

29. For Klee's stated position on the relation of the Sister Arts and his quarrel with Lessing's *Laocoon,* see ibid.

20. As quoted in Jürgen Glaesemer, *Paul Klee, Die farbige Werke im Kunstmuseum Bern* (Bern: Kornfeld und Cie, 1976), p. 30; translation my own.

31. For the relation between representation and expression or discursive and presentational forms, see Susan Langer, *Philosophy in a New Key: A Study in the Symbolism of Reason, Rite, and Art,* 3d ed. (Cambridge, Mass.: Harvard University Press, 1976), pp. 79–102.

32. See Paul Klee, *Pädagogisches Skizzenbuch* (Paris: Florian Kupferberg, 1965), pp. 6–11.

33. Klee, *Notebooks* I: 249.

34. Robert Delauney, "Ueber das Licht," translated by Paul Klee in *Der Sturm, Wochenschrift für Kultur und die Künste* 3(144/5): 255–56, 1913; reprinted in Klee, *Schriften, Rezensione und Aufsätze,* edited by Christian Geelhaar (Cologne: DuMont, 1976), p. 116; translation my own.

35. See Robert Short, *Paul Klee* (New York: W. H. Smith, 1974), p. 28.

36. Klee, *Notebooks* I: 103.

37. Blanchot, "The Absence of the Book," p. 103.

38. Franz Kafka, *Der Prozess,* in *Die Romane* (Frankfurt: Fischer, 1969), p. 436.

39. Joyce, *Finnegans Wake,* p. 107.

40. Ibid., p. 19.

41. Glaesemer, *Paul Klee,* p. 52ff.

42. See Jim M. Jordan, *Paul Klee and Cubism* (Princeton, N.J.: Princeton University Press, 1984), pp. 82–115.

43. See Loren Eitner, "The Open Window and the Storm-Tossed Boat," *Art Bulletin* 37: 281–90, 1955.

44. See Erwin Panofsky, *Early Netherlandish Painting* (New York: Harper and Row, 1953), I: 3–4.

45. Klee, *Notebooks,* I: 51–52.

46. Derrida, "Ellipses," in *Writing and Difference,* p. 296.

Index

BLUNDESTON